EASY PIANO

ROGUE ONE
A STAR WARS STORY™

MUSIC FROM THE MOTION PICTURE SOUNDTRACK

ISBN 978-1-4950-8989-3

DISTRIBUTED BY

7777 W. BLUEMOUND RD. P.O. BOX 13819 MILWAUKEE, WI 53213

In Australia Contact:
Hal Leonard Australia Pty. Ltd.
4 Lentara Court
Cheltenham, Victoria, 3192 Australia
Email: ausadmin@halleonard.com.au

Visit Hal Leonard Online at
www.halleonard.com

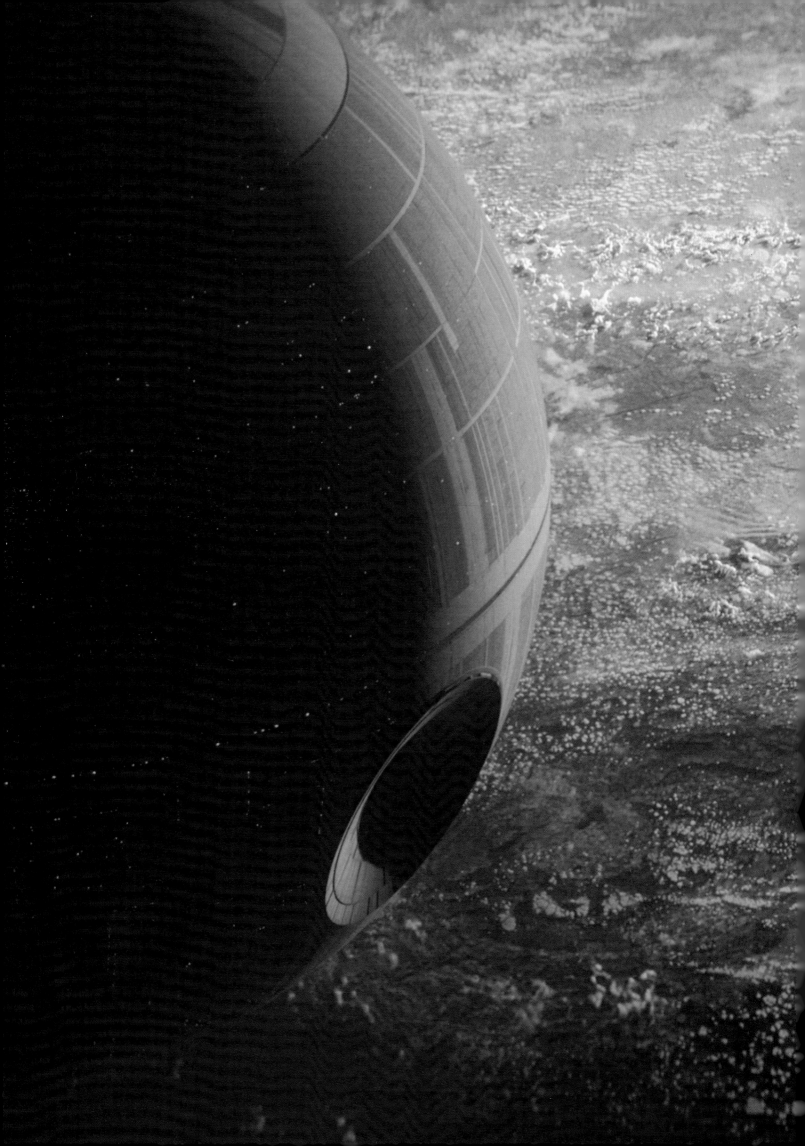

CONTENTS

HE'S HERE FOR US

Music by MICHAEL GIACCHINO

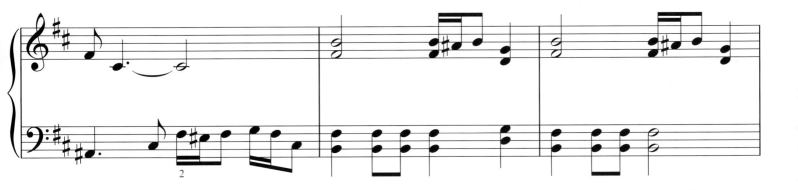

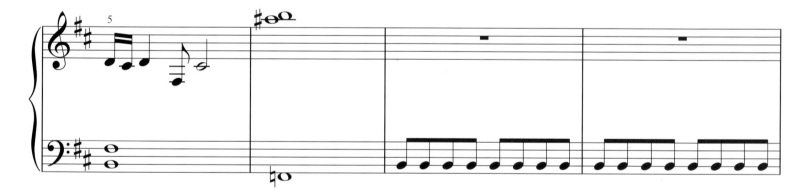

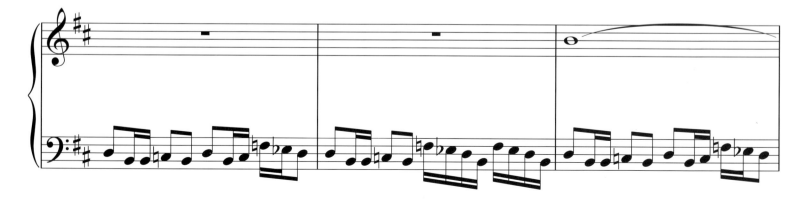

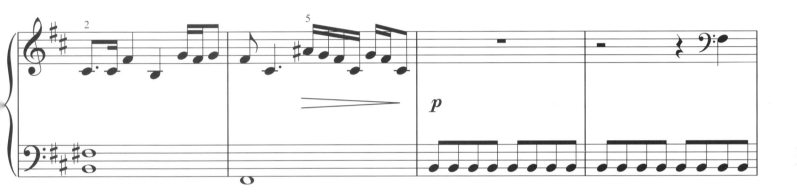

A LONG RIDE AHEAD

Music by MICHAEL GIACCHINO

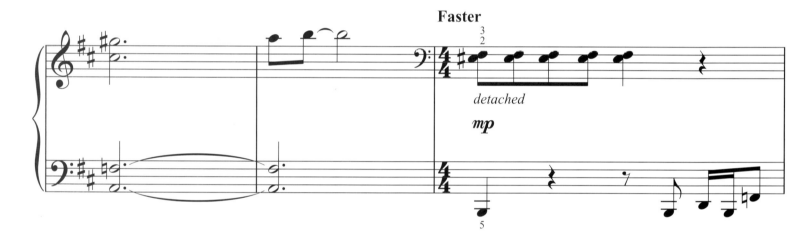

Slowly, expressively

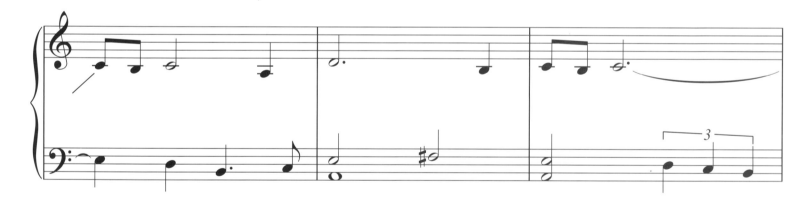

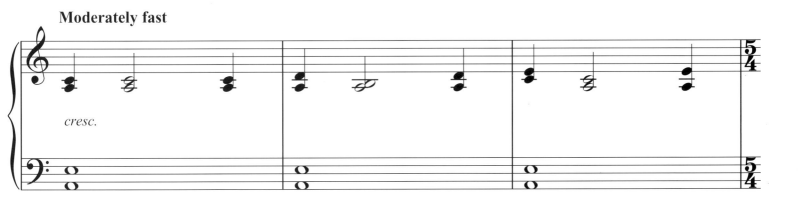

Moderately fast

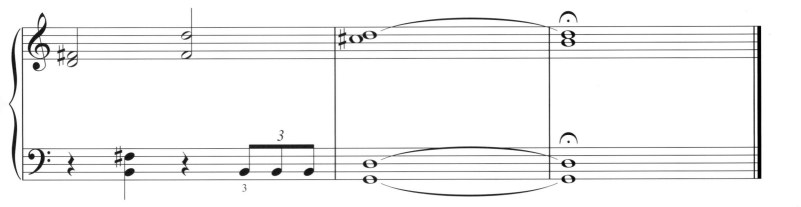

WOBANI IMPERIAL LABOR CAMP

Music by MICHAEL GIACCHINO

Moderately slow

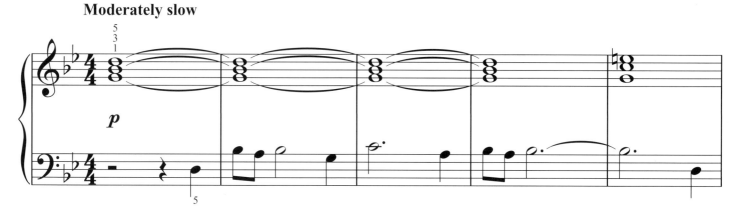

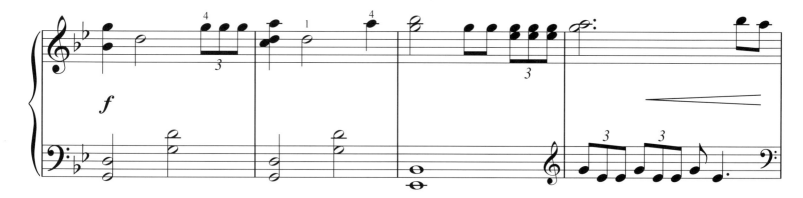

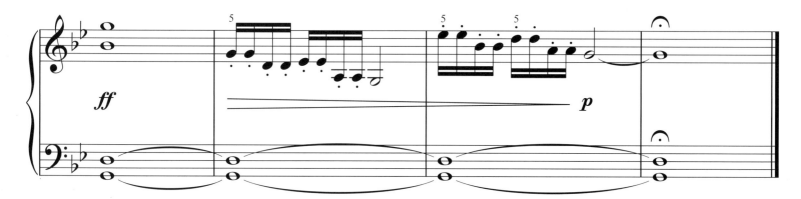

TRUST GOES BOTH WAYS

Music by MICHAEL GIACCHINO

Moderately

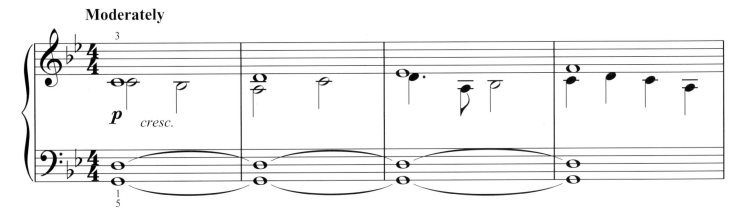

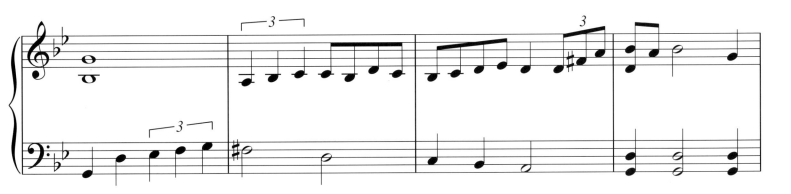

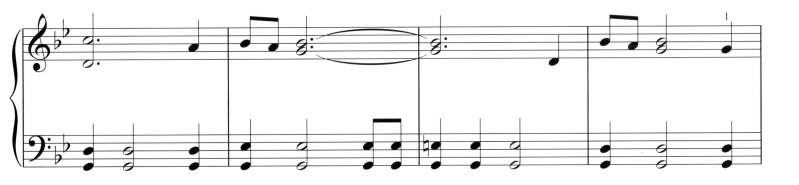

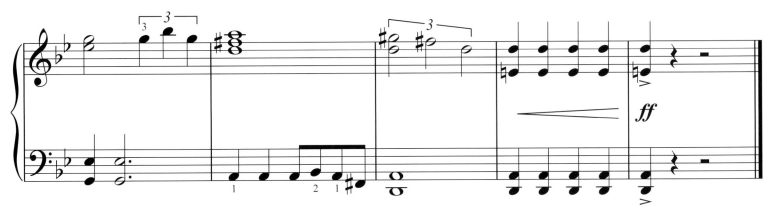

JEDHA ARRIVAL

Music by MICHAEL GIACCHINO

Moderately slow

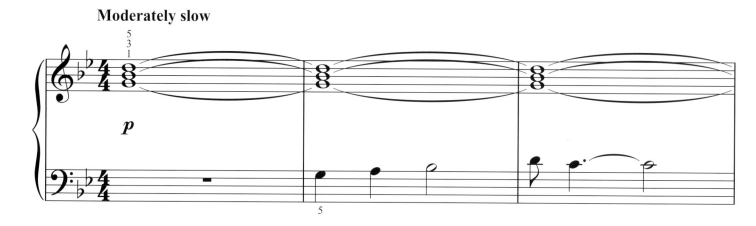

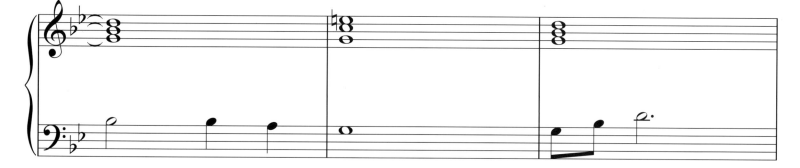

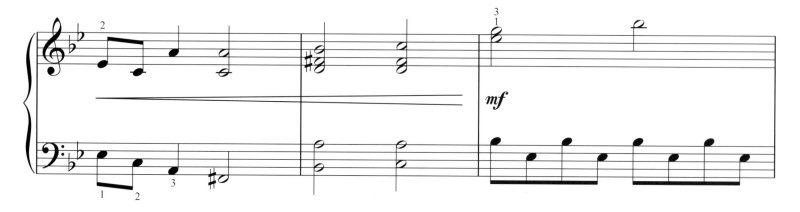

Twice as fast

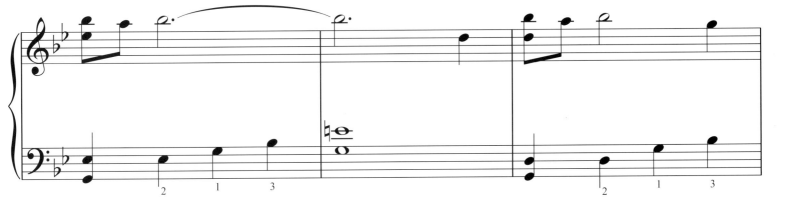

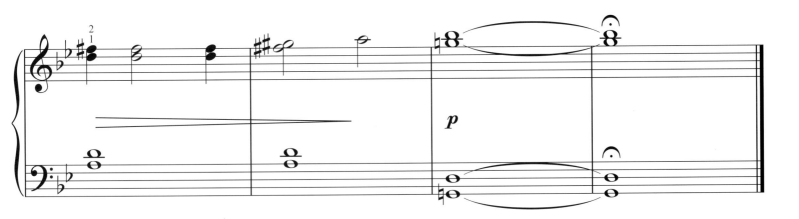

CONFRONTATION ON EADU

Music by MICHAEL GIACCHINO

Very slowly

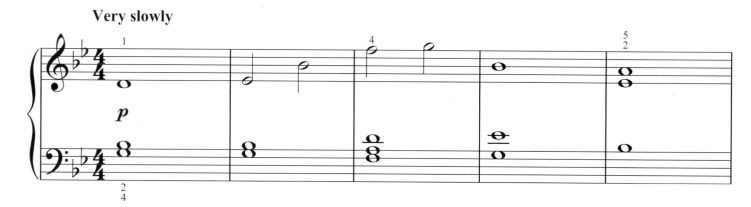

Moderately

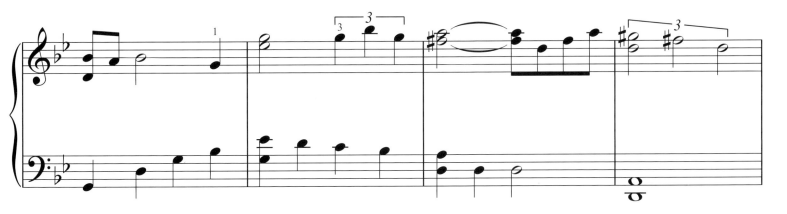

Faster

Moderately fast

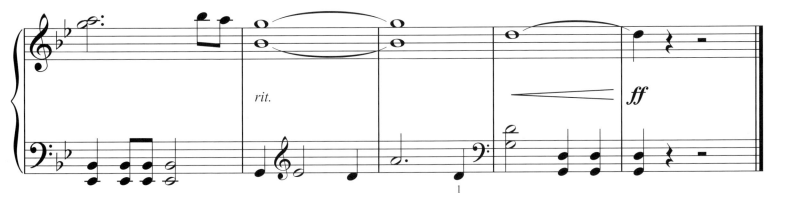

REBELLIONS ARE BUILT ON HOPE

Music by MICHAEL GIACCHINO

Slowly

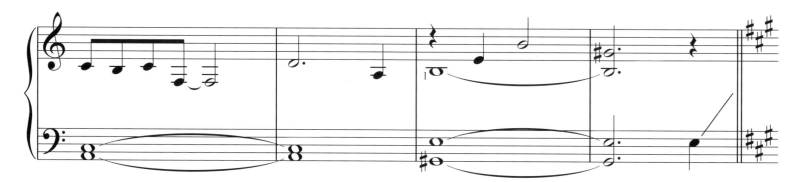

Slightly faster

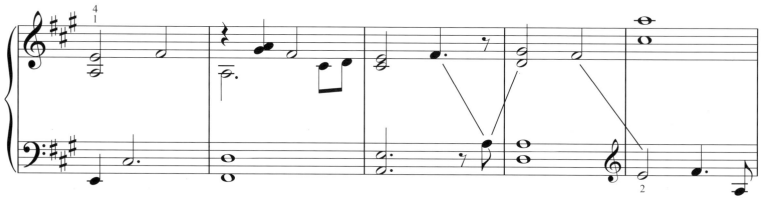

Quickly

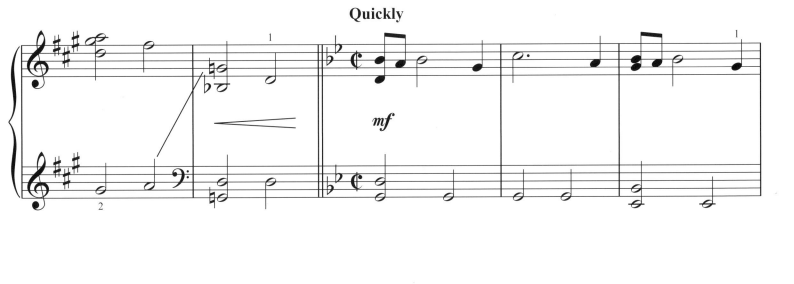

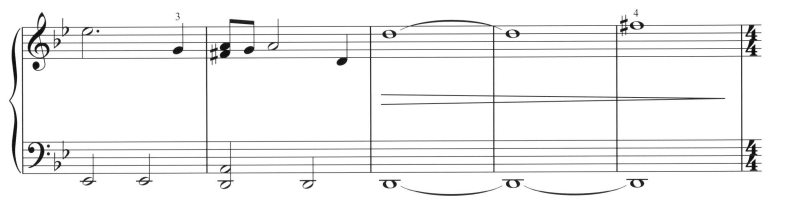

Slowly

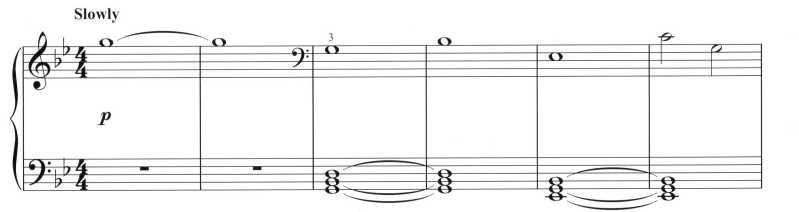

ROGUE ONE

Music by MICHAEL GIACCHINO

Briskly

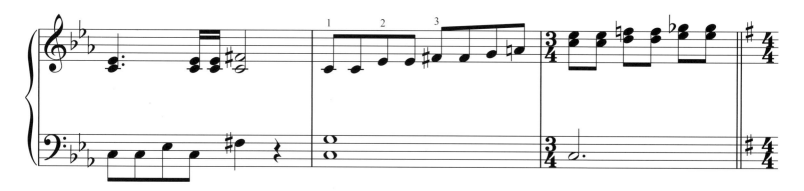

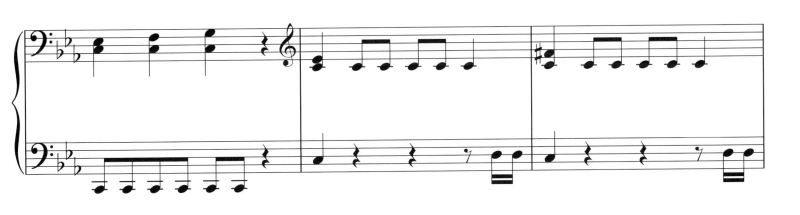

YOUR FATHER WOULD BE PROUD

Music by MICHAEL GIACCHINO

Slowly, expressively

cresc.

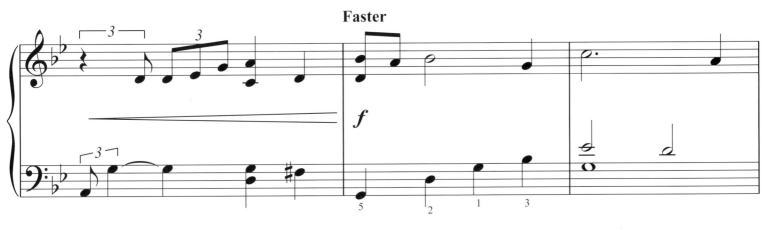

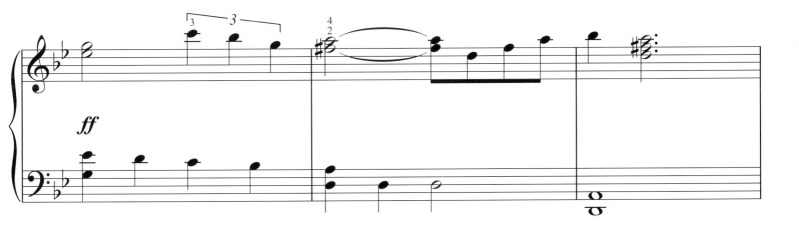

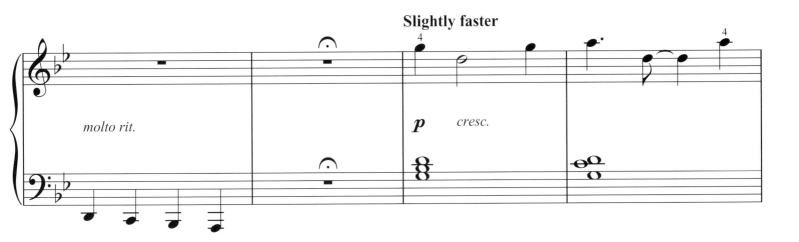

Moderately fast

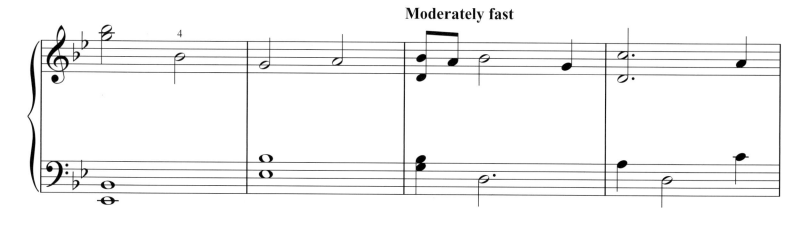

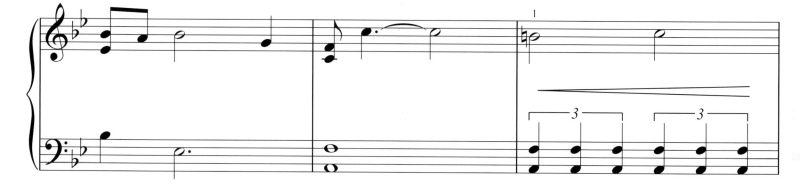

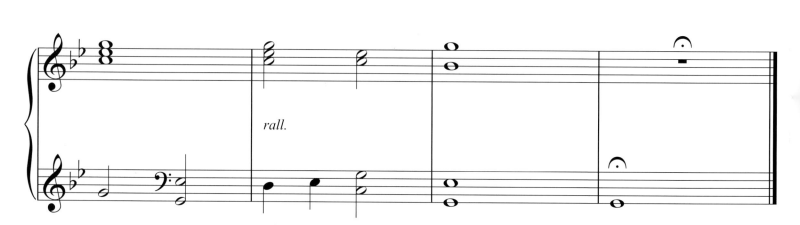

THE IMPERIAL SUITE

Music by MICHAEL GIACCHINO

Moderately, in 2

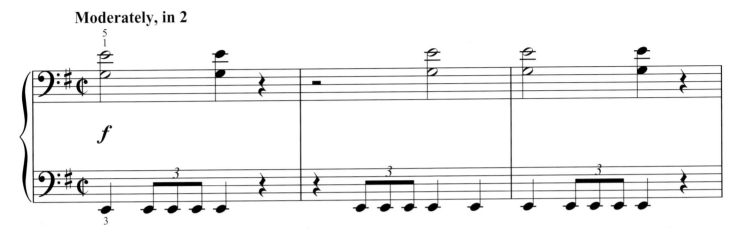

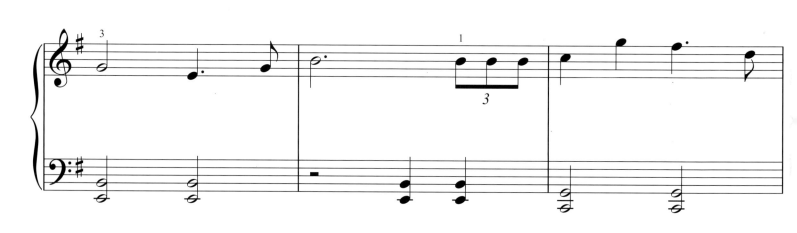

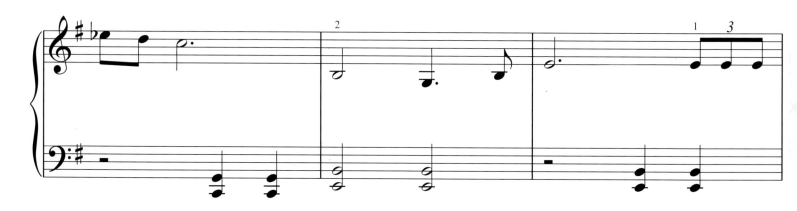

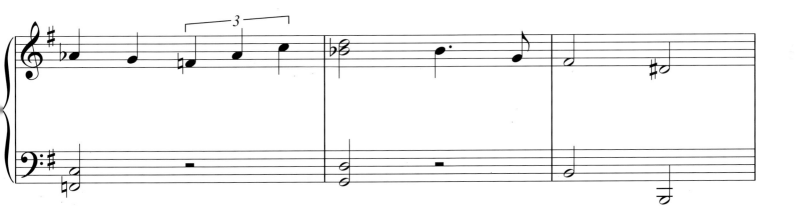

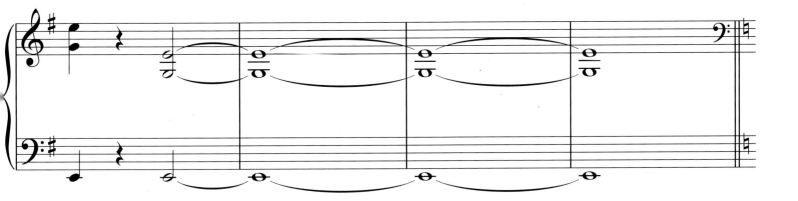

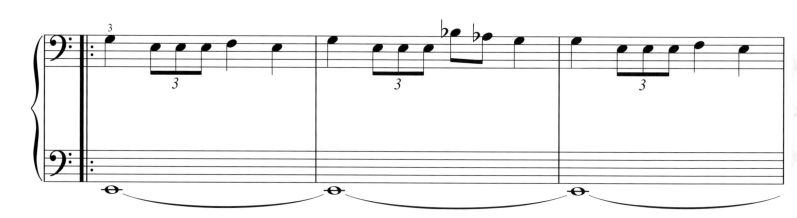

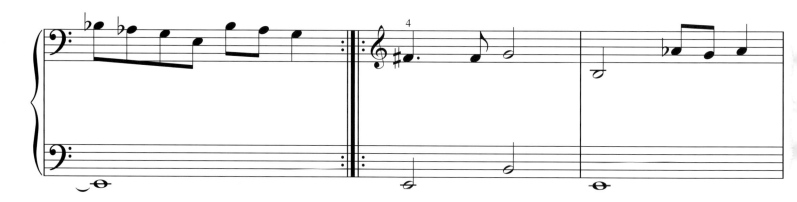

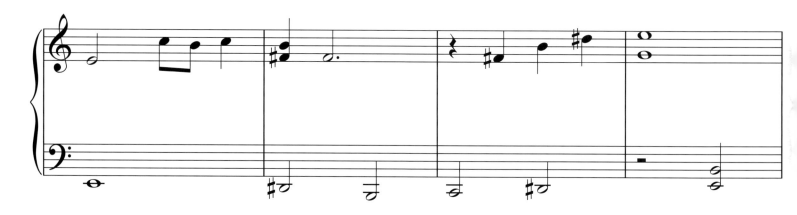

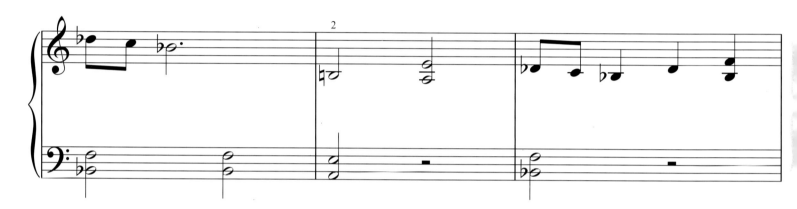

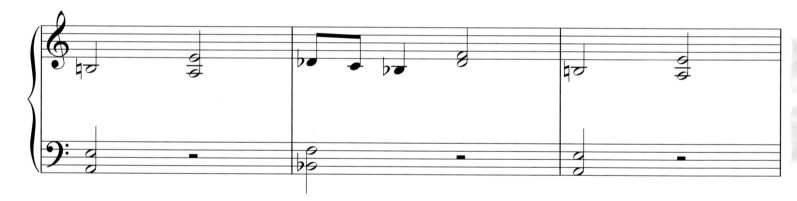

GUITAR NOTATION LEGEND

THE MUSICAL STAFF shows pitches and rhythms and is divided by bar lines into measures. Pitches are named after the first seven letters of the alphabet.

TABLATURE graphically represents the guitar fingerboard. Each horizontal line represents a string, and each number represents a fret.

4th string, 2nd fret

1st & 2nd strings open, played together

open D chord

HALF-STEP BEND: Strike the note and bend up 1/2 step.

WHOLE-STEP BEND: Strike the note and bend up one step.

GRACE NOTE BEND: Strike the note and immediately bend up as indicated.

SLIGHT (MICROTONE) BEND: Strike the note and bend up 1/4 step.

BEND AND RELEASE: Strike the note and bend up as indicated, then release back to the original note. Only the first note is struck.

PRE-BEND: Bend the note as indicated, then strike it.

VIBRATO: The string is vibrated by rapidly bending and releasing the note with the fretting hand.

PALM MUTING: The note is partially muted by the pick hand lightly touching the string(s) just before the bridge.

HAMMER-ON: Strike the first (lower) note with one finger, then sound the higher note (on the same string) with another finger by fretting it without picking.

PULL-OFF: Place both fingers on the notes to be sounded. Strike the first note and without picking, pull the finger off to sound the second (lower) note.

LEGATO SLIDE: Strike the first note and then slide the same fret-hand finger up or down to the second note. The second note is not struck.

SHIFT SLIDE: Same as legato slide, except the second note is struck.

TRILL: Very rapidly alternate between the notes indicated by continuously hammering on and pulling off.

TAPPING: Hammer ("tap") the fret indicated with the pick-hand index or middle finger and pull off to the note fretted by the fret hand.

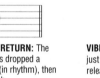

NATURAL HARMONIC: Strike the note while the fret-hand lightly touches the string directly over the fret indicated.

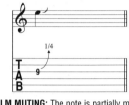

PINCH HARMONIC: The note is fretted normally and a harmonic is produced by adding the edge of the thumb or the tip of the index finger of the pick hand to the normal pick attack.

TREMOLO PICKING: The note is picked as rapidly and continuously as possible.

VIBRATO BAR DIVE AND RETURN: The pitch of the note or chord is dropped a specified number of steps (in rhythm), then returned to the original pitch.

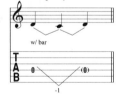

VIBRATO BAR SCOOP: Depress the bar just before striking the note, then quickly release the bar.

VIBRATO BAR DIP: Strike the note and then immediately drop a specified number of steps, then release back to the original pitch.

Additional Musical Definitions

(accent)

• Accentuate note (play it louder).

(staccato)

• Play the note short.

D.S. al Coda

• Go back to the sign (𝄋), then play until the measure marked "***To Coda***," then skip to the section labelled "**Coda**."

D.C. al Fine

• Go back to the beginning of the song and play until the measure marked "***Fine***" (end).

Fill

N.C.

• Label used to identify a brief melodic figure which is to be inserted into the arrangement.

• Harmony is implied.

• Repeat measures between signs.

• When a repeated section has different endings, play the first ending only the first time and the second ending only the second time.

CONTENTS

All Summer Long

Words and Music by Ronnie Van Zant, Ed King, Gary Rossington, Warren Zevon,
Robert Wachtel, LeRoy Marinel, Matthew Shafer and Robert Ritchie

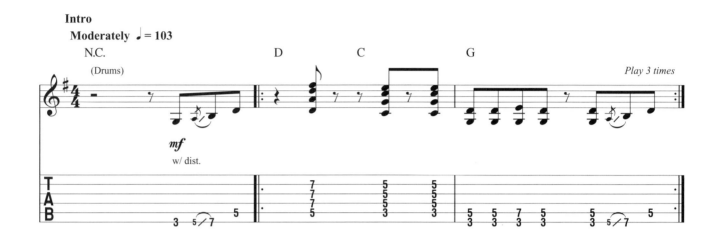

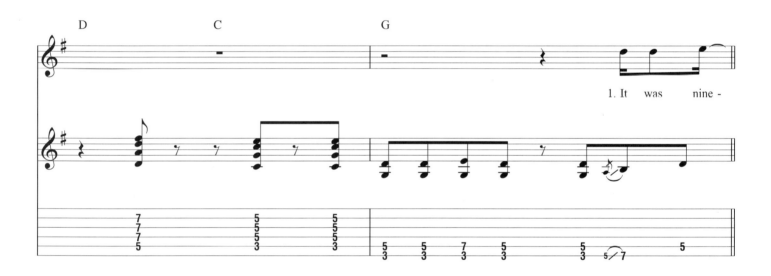

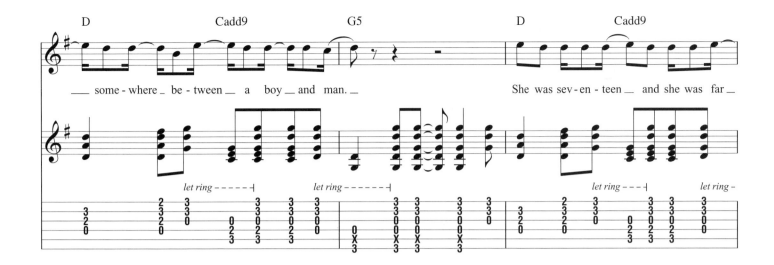

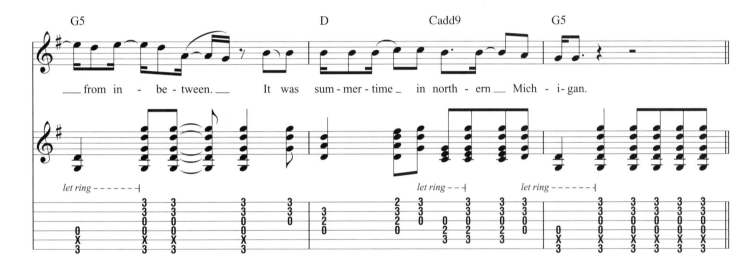

Interlude

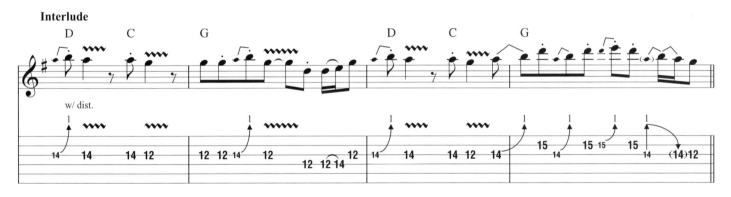

Verse

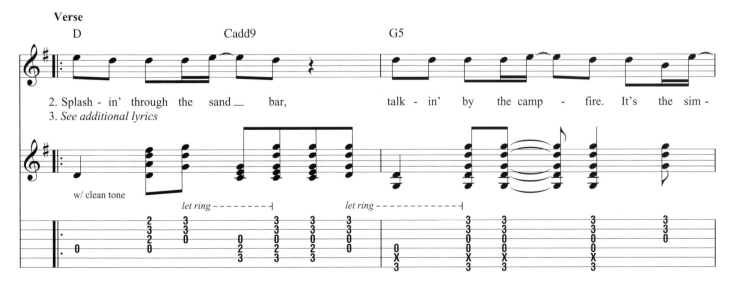

2. Splash - in' through the sand bar, talk - in' by the camp - fire. It's the sim -
3. *See additional lyrics*

w/ clean tone

5

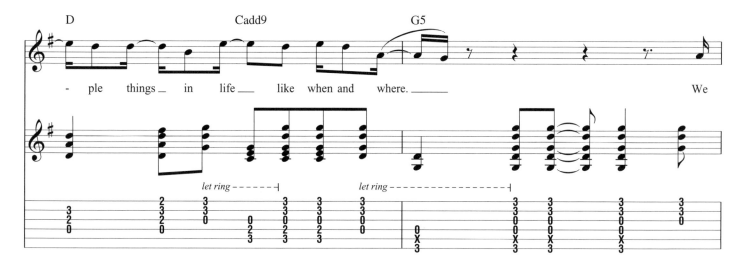

-ple things _ in life _ like when and where. _ We

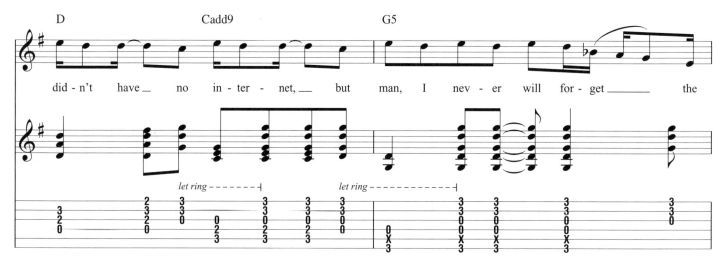

did - n't have _ no in - ter - net, _ but man, I nev - er will for - get _ the

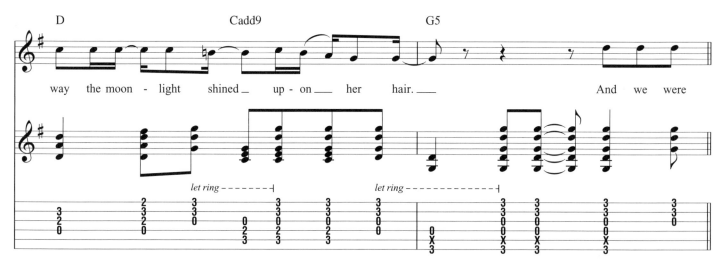

way the moon - light shined _ up - on _ her hair. _ And we were

Chorus

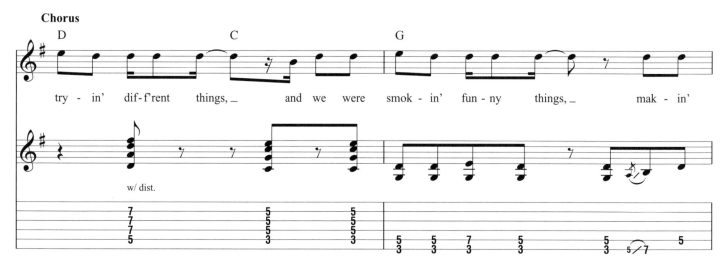

try - in' dif - f'rent things, _ and we were smok - in' fun - ny things, _ mak - in'

w/ dist.

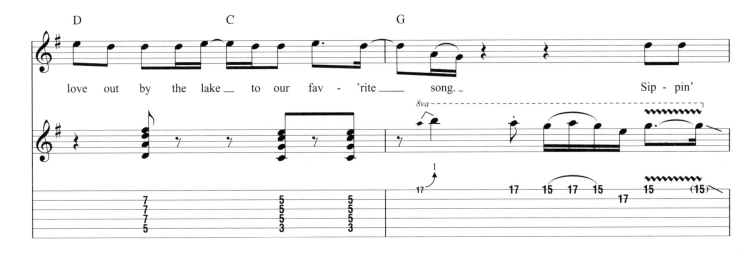

love out by the lake __ to our fav - 'rite ____ song. __   Sip - pin'

whis - key out the bot - tle,   not think - in' 'bout to - mor - row, sing - in' "Sweet __

____ Home Al - a - bam - a" ____ all   sum - mer   long. __

Interlude

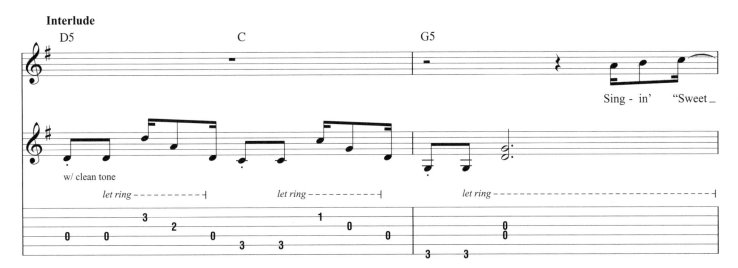

Sing - in' "Sweet __

w/ clean tone

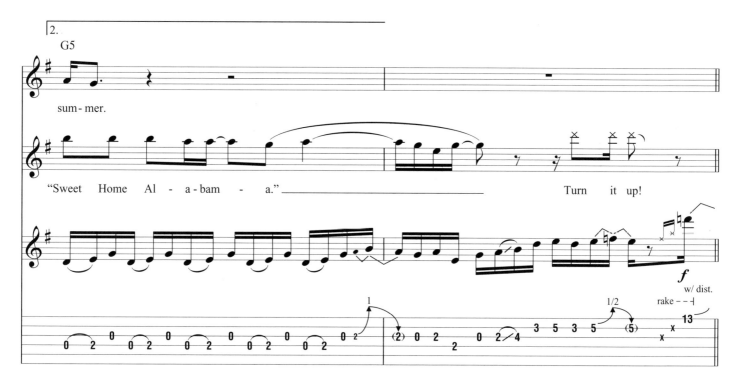

Guitar Solo

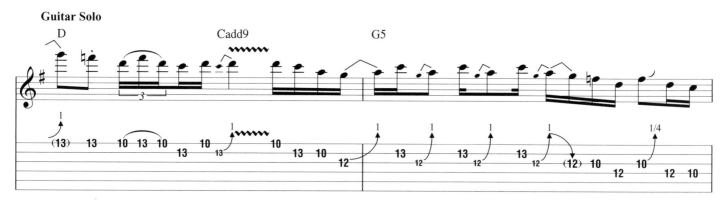

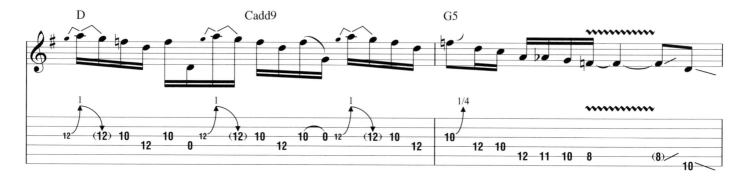

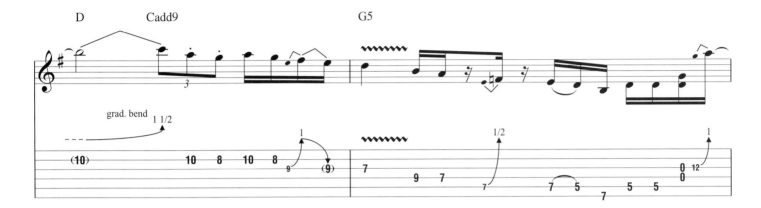

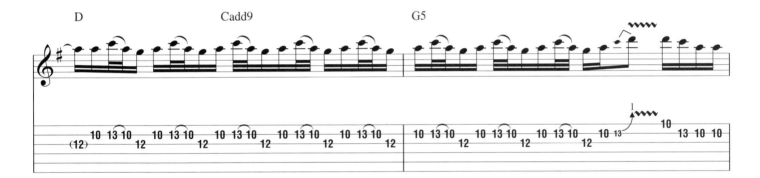

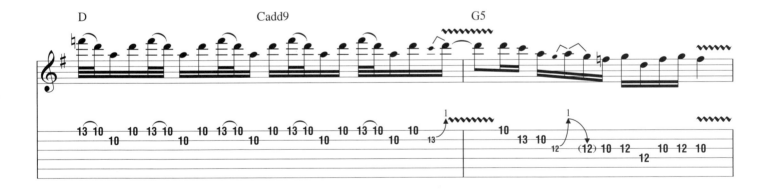

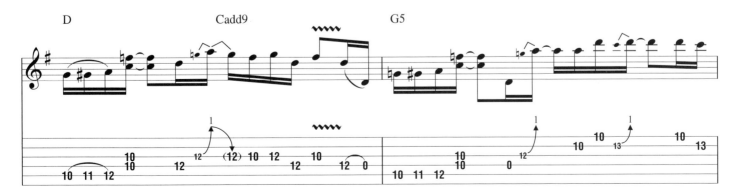

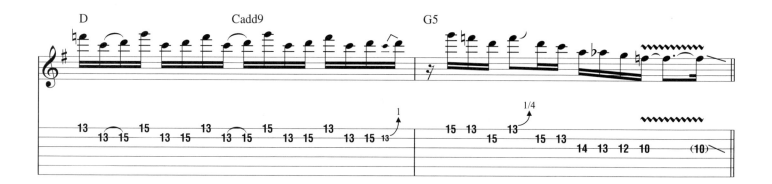

Interlude

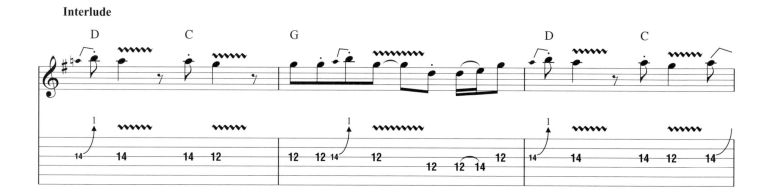

Verse

4. Now, noth-in' seems as strange as when the leaves

w/ clean tone

let ring

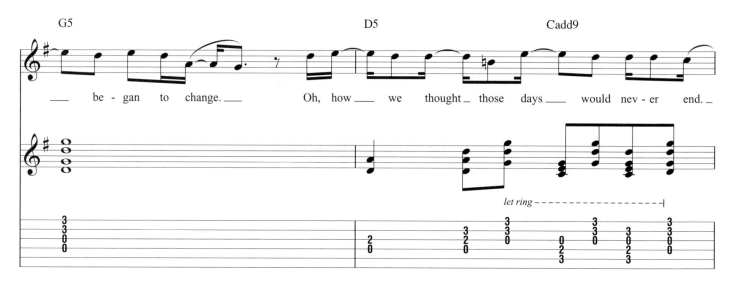

be - gan to change. Oh, how we thought those days would nev - er end.

let ring

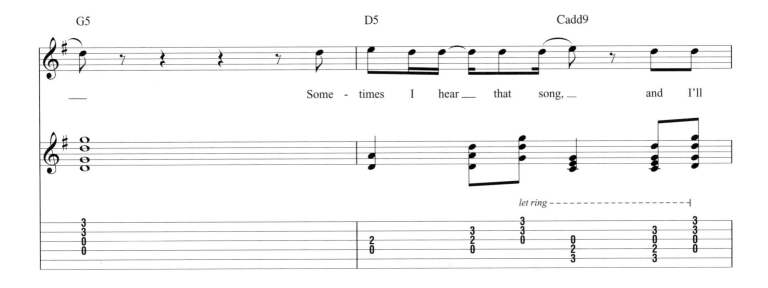

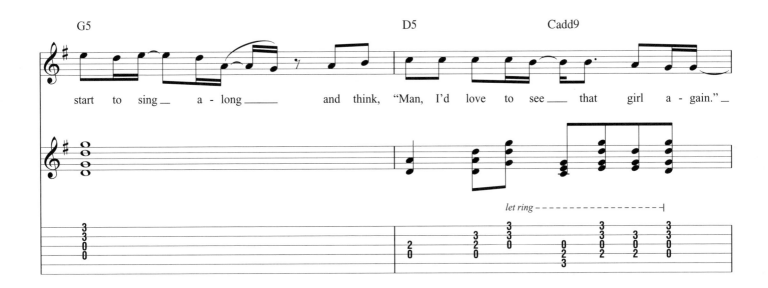

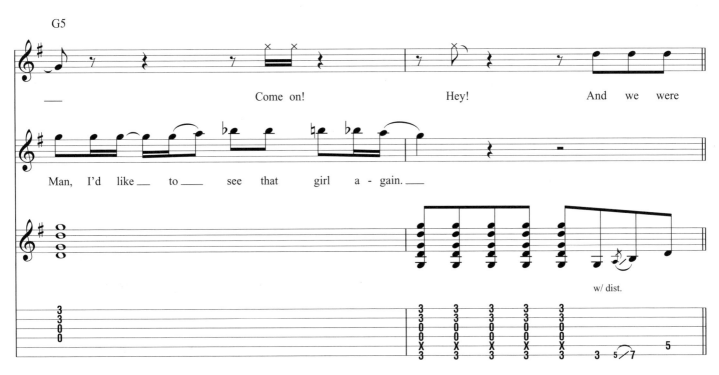

Chorus

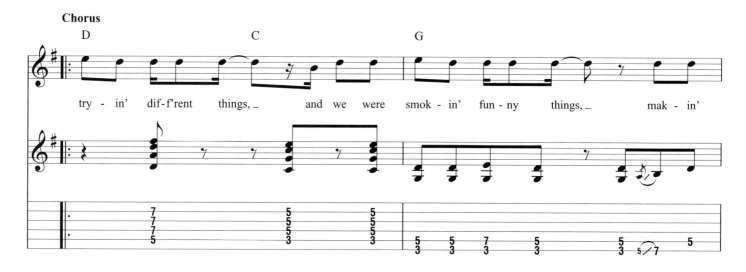

try - in' dif-f'rent things, _ and we were smok - in' fun - ny things, _ mak - in'

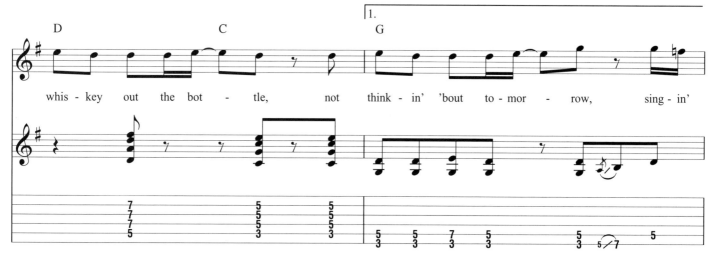

love out by the lake _ to our fav - 'rite _ song. _ Sip - pin'

1.

whis - key out the bot - tle, not think - in' 'bout to - mor - row, sing - in'

"Sweet Home Al - a - bam - a" all _ sum - mer _ long. We were

think - in' 'bout to - mor - row, sing - in' "Sweet __ Home Al - a - bam - a" _____ all

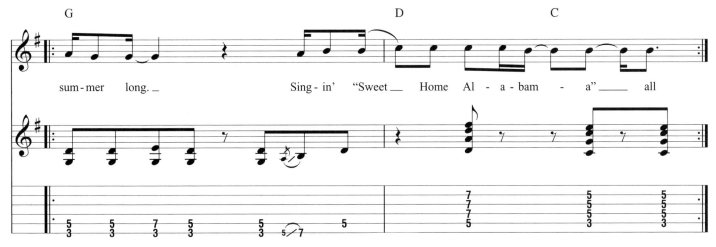

sum - mer long. _ Sing - in' "Sweet __ Home Al - a - bam - a" _____ all

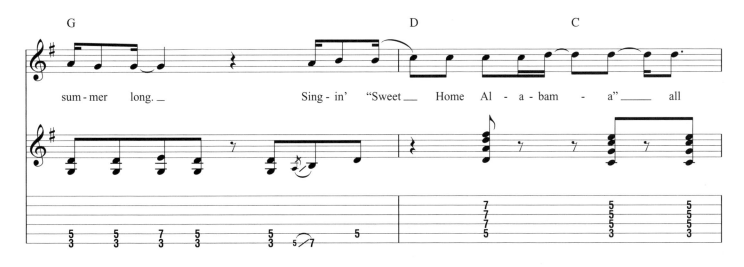

sum - mer long. _ Sing - in' "Sweet __ Home Al - a - bam - a" _____ all

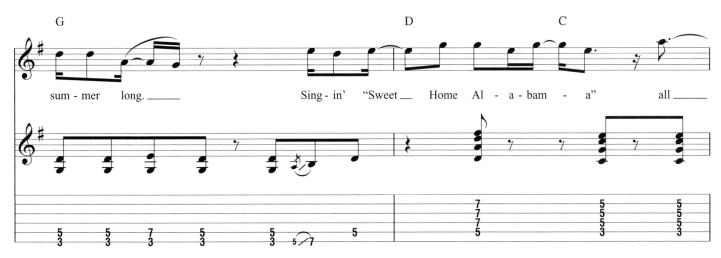

sum - mer long. _____ Sing - in' "Sweet __ Home Al - a - bam - a" all _____

Outro

Additional Lyrics

3. Catchin' walleye from the dock, watchin' the waves roll off the rocks.
She'll forever hold a spot inside my soul.
We'd blister in the sun, we couldn't wait for night to come
To hit that sand and play some rock and roll. While we were...

Chicken Fried

Words and Music by Zac Brown and Wyatt Durrette

Tune down 1/2 step:
(low to high) Eb-Ab-Db-Gb-Bb-Eb

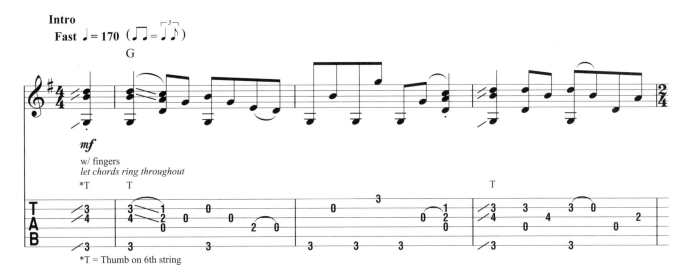

*T = Thumb on 6th string

You know I like my

Chorus

chick-en fried, ____ and cold beer on a Fri-day night, _ a pair of jeans that fit _

__ just right, and the ra-di-o up. _____

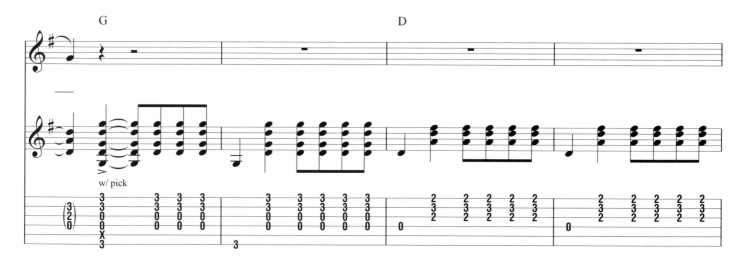

w/ pick

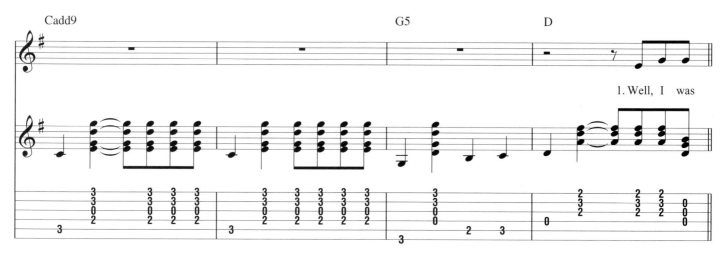

1. Well, I was

Verse

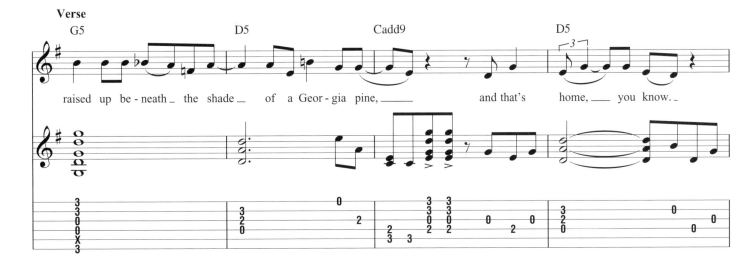

raised up be - neath — the shade — of a Geor - gia pine, _____ and that's home, ___ you know. _

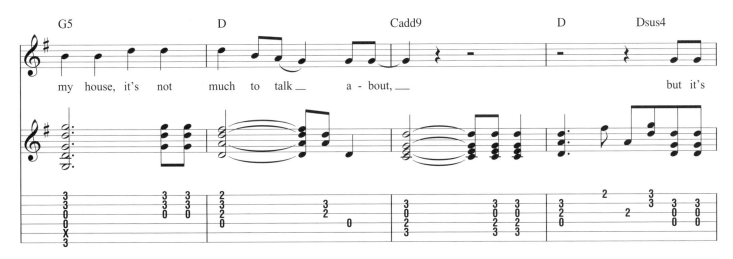

Sweet tea, pe - can pie, ___ and home - made _ wine ___ where the peach - es grow. _ And

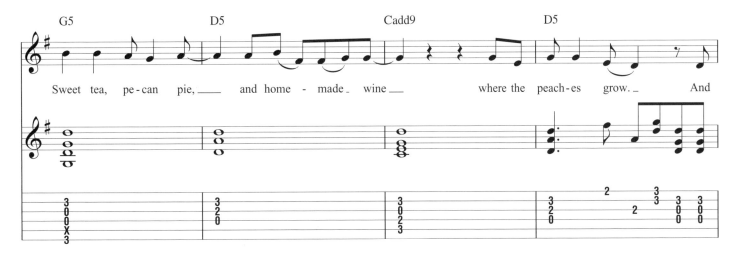

my house, it's not much to talk __ a - bout, __ but it's

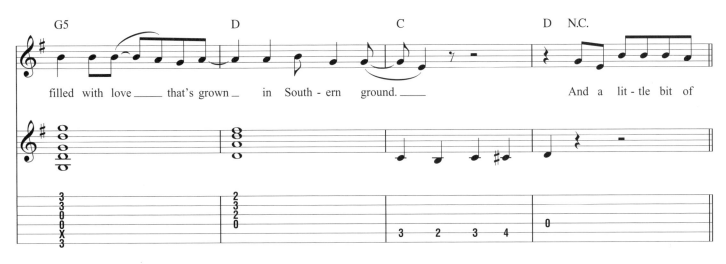

filled with love _____ that's grown ___ in South - ern ground. ___ And a lit - tle bit of

chick-en fried, ___ cold beer on a Fri-day night, ___ a pair of jeans that fit ___

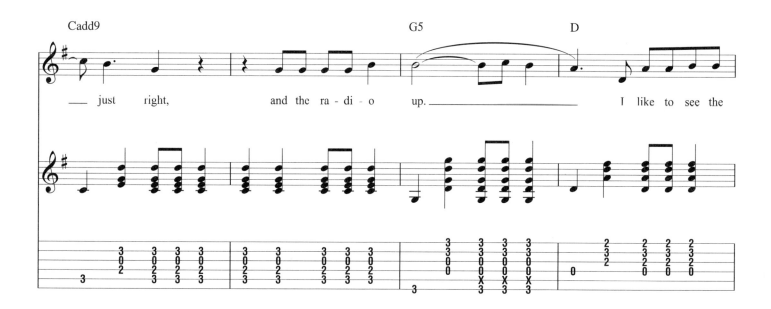

___ just right, and the ra-di-o up. ___ I like to see the

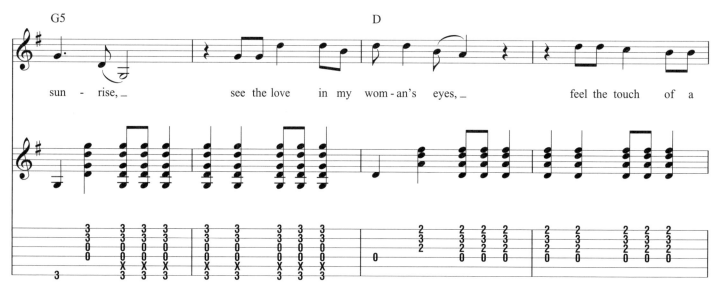

sun - rise, ___ see the love in my wom-an's eyes, ___ feel the touch of a

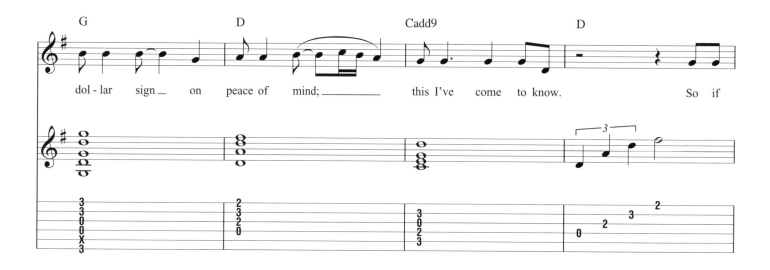

dol - lar sign __ on peace of mind; _____ this I've come to know. So if

D.S. al Coda 1

you a - gree, _ have a drink with me; _ raise your glass - es for a toast __ to a lit - tle bit of

Coda 1

Fiddle Solo

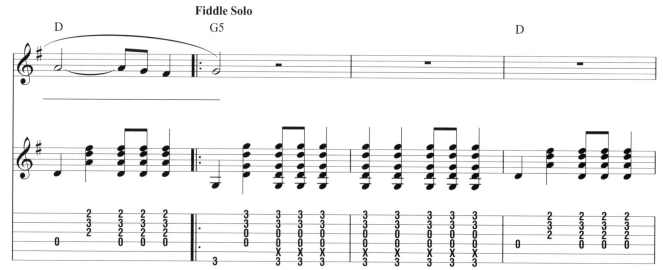

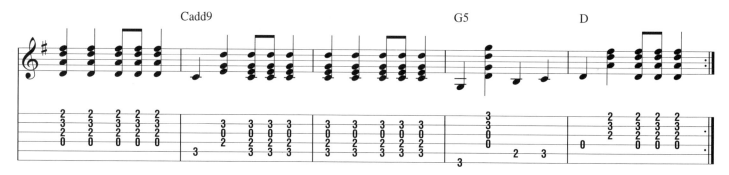

Interlude

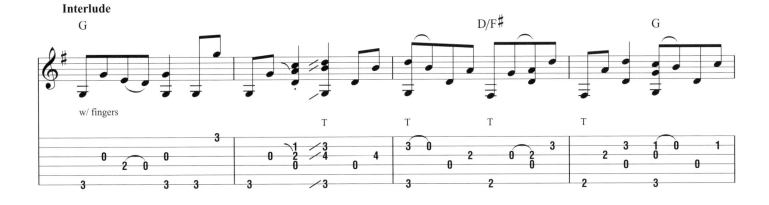

Verse

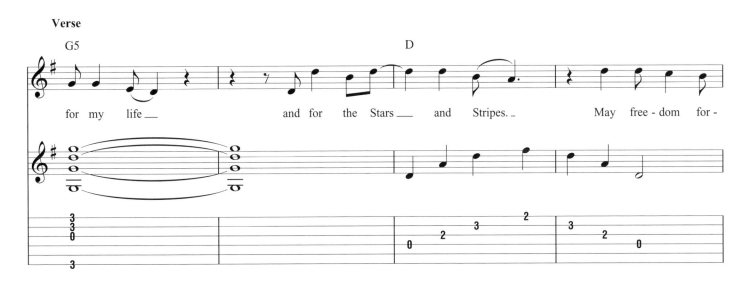

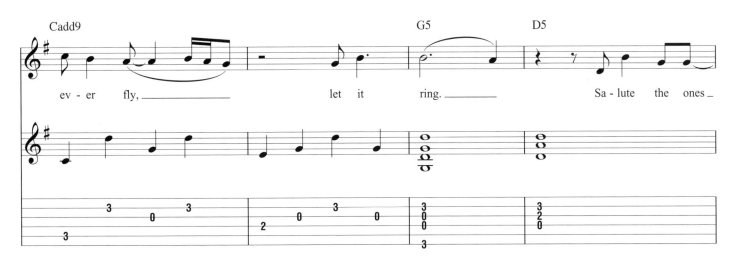

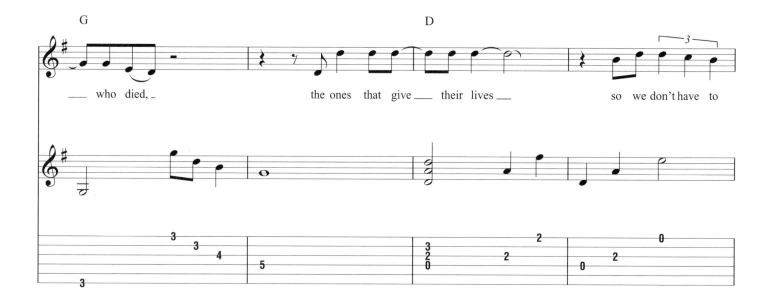

who died, — the ones that give — their lives — so we don't have to

sac - ri - fice — all the things we love. — Like our

D.S. al Coda 2

⊕ Coda 2

Outro-Chorus

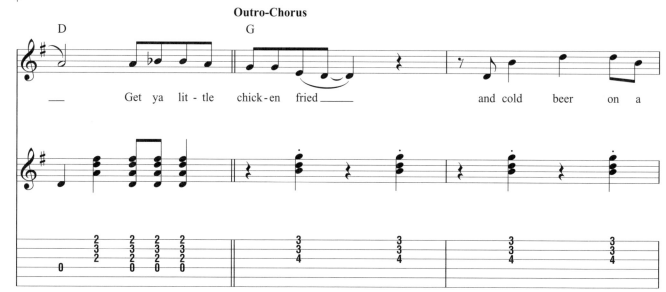

— Get ya lit - tle chick-en fried — and cold beer on a

22

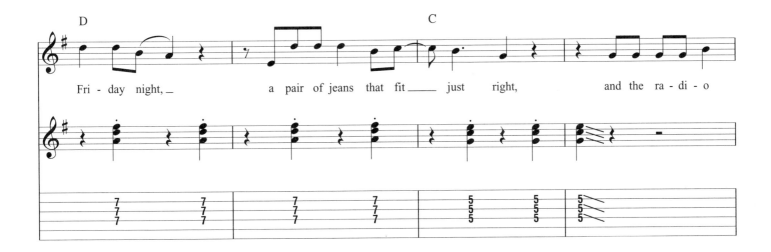

Fri - day night, _ a pair of jeans that fit _ just right, and the ra - di - o

up. _ I like to see the sun - rise, _ see the love in my

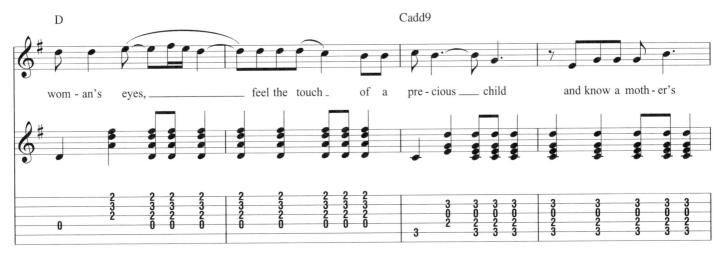

wom - an's eyes, _ feel the touch _ of a pre - cious _ child and know a moth - er's

love. _

Country Girl
(Shake It for Me)

Words and Music by Luke Bryan and Dallas Davidson

Intro

Moderate Country ♩ = 106

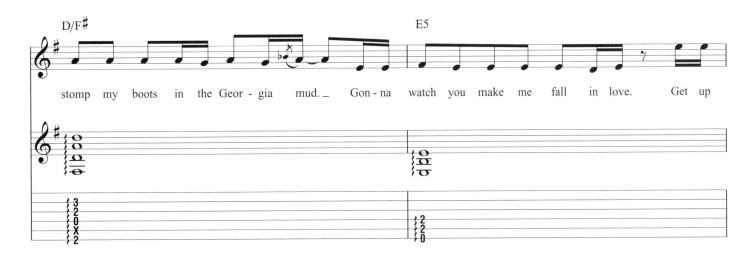

Verse

crick-ets and the crit-ters and the squir-rels. Shake it to the moon, _ shake it for me, girl, aw. _

𝄋 Chorus

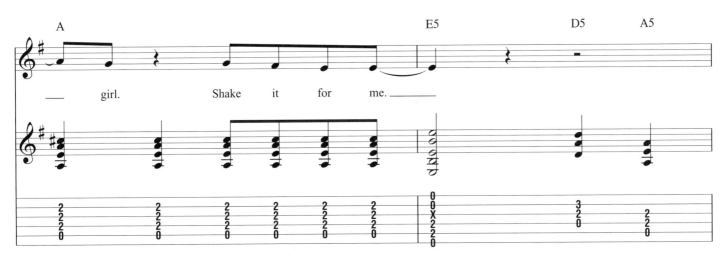

Coun - try girl, shake it for me, _____ girl. Shake it for me, _

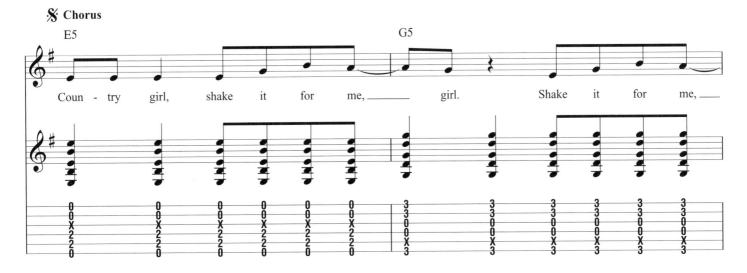

_ girl. Shake it for me. _____

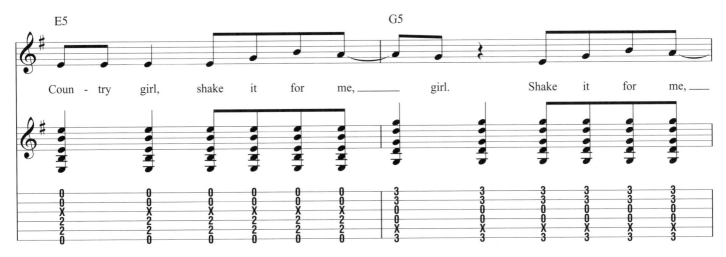

Coun - try girl, shake it for me, _____ girl. Shake it for me, _

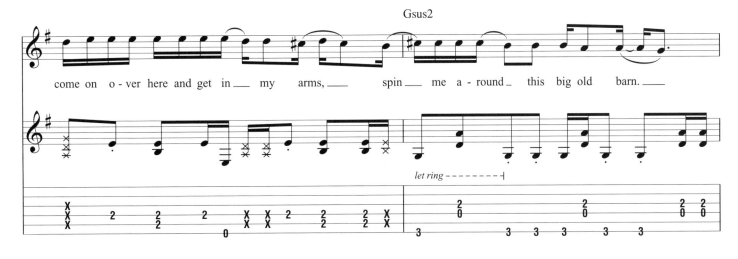

Gsus2

come on o-ver here and get in my arms, spin me a-round this big old barn.

D/F#   Em7

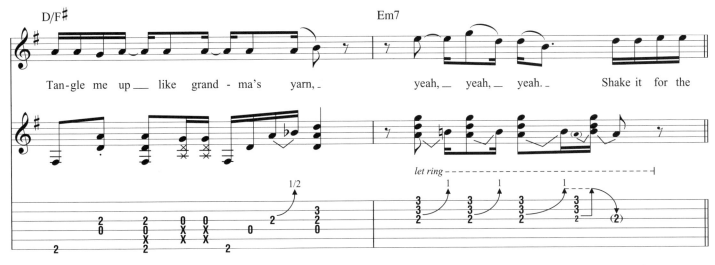

Tan-gle me up like grand-ma's yarn, yeah, yeah, yeah. Shake it for the

Pre-Chorus

E5   G6

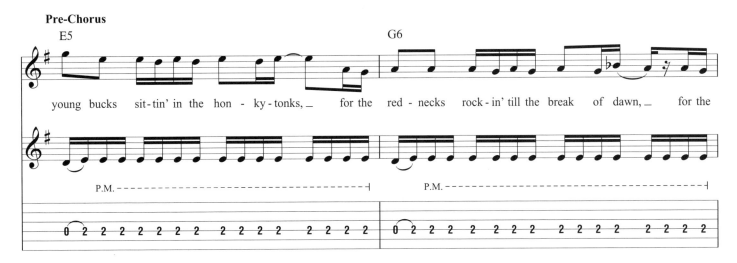

young bucks sit-tin' in the hon-ky-tonks, for the red-necks rock-in' till the break of dawn, for the

Dsus2/F#   E5

D - J spin-nin' that coun-try song. Come on, come on, come on. Shake it for the

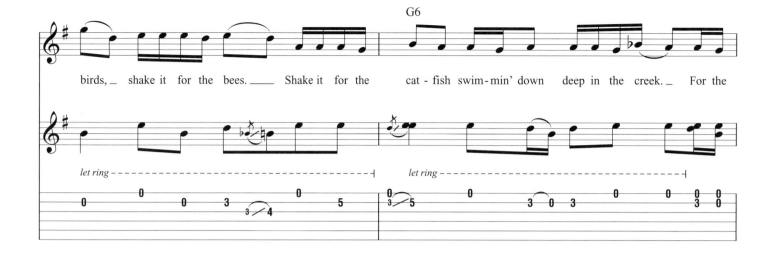

birds, __ shake it for the bees. __ Shake it for the cat - fish swim-min' down deep in the creek. __ For the

D.S. al Coda 1

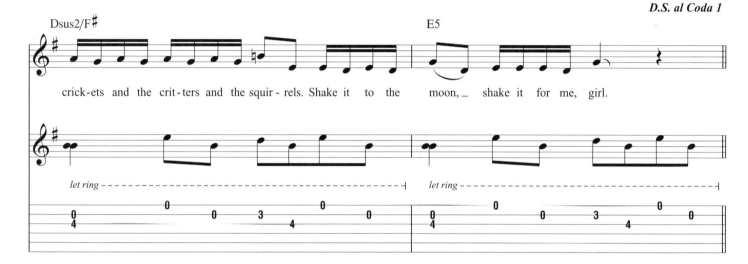

crick-ets and the crit-ters and the squir-rels. Shake it to the moon, __ shake it for me, girl.

⊕ Coda 1

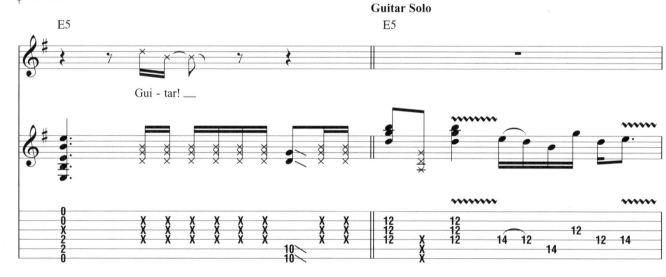

Guitar Solo

Gui - tar! __

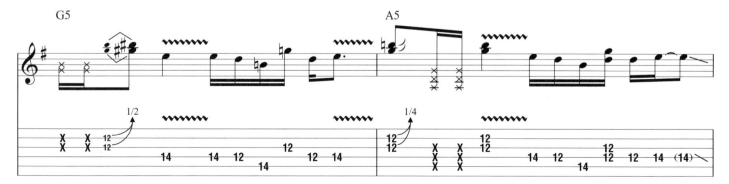

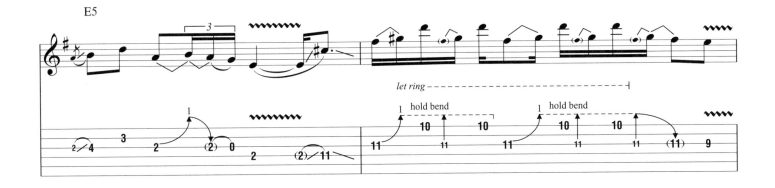

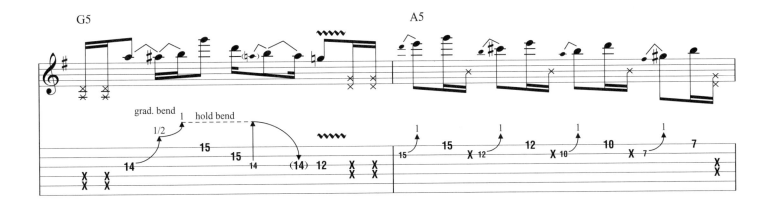

Bridge

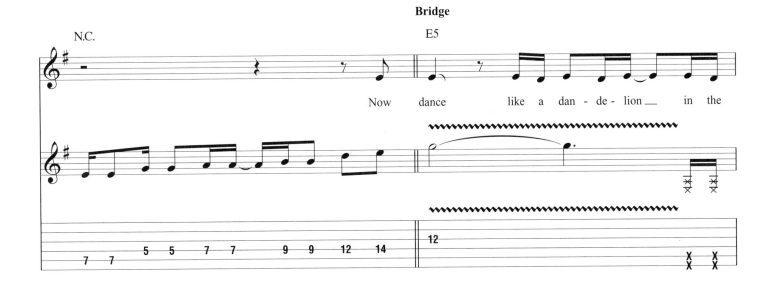

Now   dance   like   a   dan - de - lion__   in   the

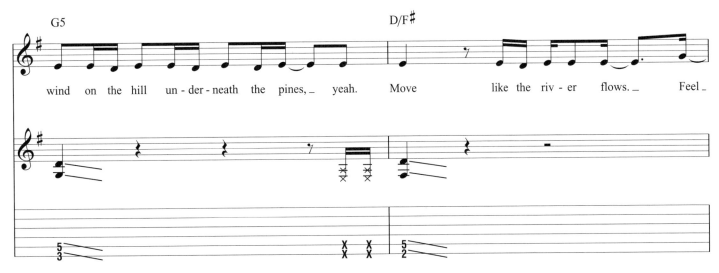

wind   on   the   hill   un - der - neath   the   pines,__   yeah.   Move   like   the   riv - er   flows.__   Feel__

Pre-Chorus

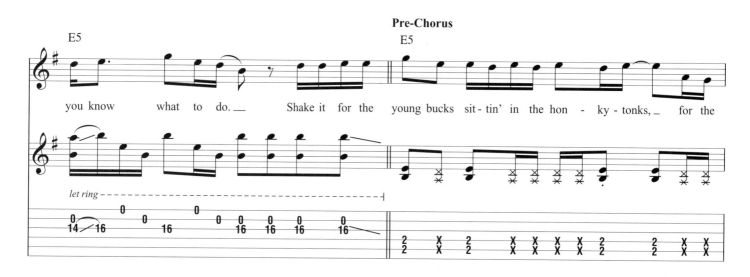

___ come on, __ come on. __ Shake it for the birds, __ shake it for the bees. ____ Shake it for the_

_cat - fish swim- min' down deep in the creek, _ for the crick - ets and the crit - ters and the squir - rels. Shake it to the_

D.S. al Coda 2   **Coda 2**

_moon, _ shake it for me, girl, aw._

Coun-try girl, __ shake it for me, ____ girl. __ Shake it for me, ____ girl. __ Shake it for me. __

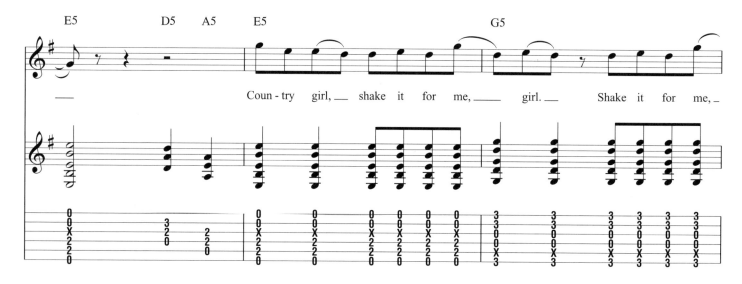

__ Coun-try girl, __ shake it for me, ____ girl. __ Shake it for me, __

__ girl. __ Shake it for me. _____

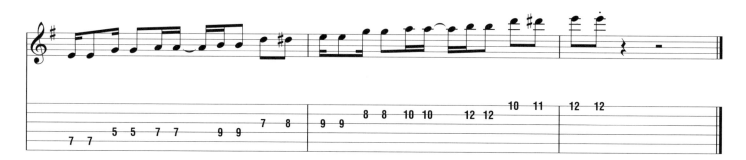

Done

Words and Music by Reid Perry, Neil Perry, Jacob Bryant and John Davidson

Tune down 1/2 step:
(low to high) Eb-Ab-Db-Gb-Bb-Eb

Mm. _____

Oo, ___ hoo, oo,

oo,   hoo. _____ Yeah, _____ yeah. _____   1. You've been

Verse

wear-ing that crown and tear - ing me down. _ It's been a while since you've treat-ed me right. _   You

w/ clean tone

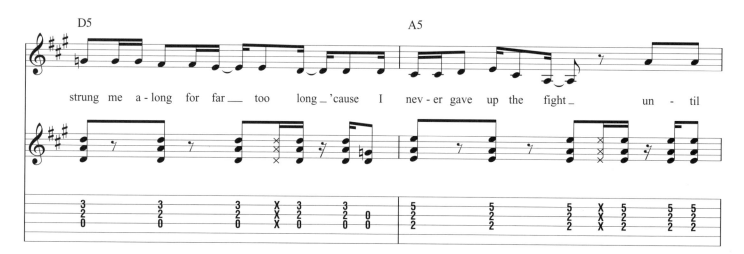

strung me a-long for far _ too long _ 'cause I nev-er gave up the fight _ un - til

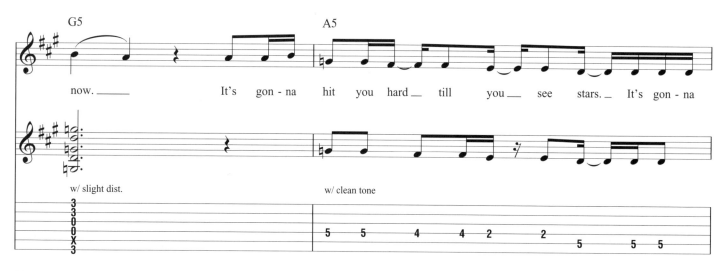

now. _____   It's gon-na hit you hard _ till you _ see stars. _ It's gon-na

w/ slight dist.   w/ clean tone

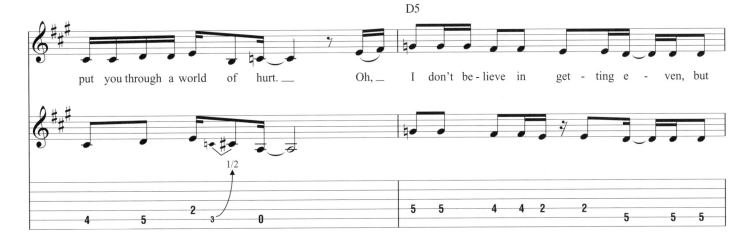

Chorus

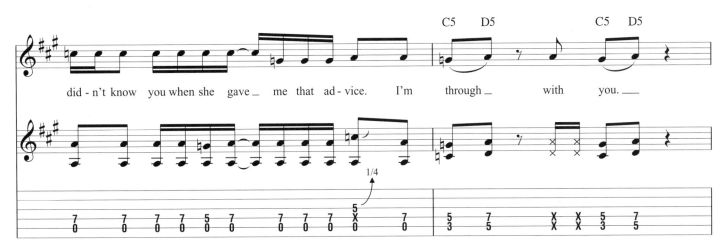

You're one bridge I'd like to burn, {1., 2. bot - tle up the ash - es, / 3. scat - ter the ash - es,} smash the urn. And I'm

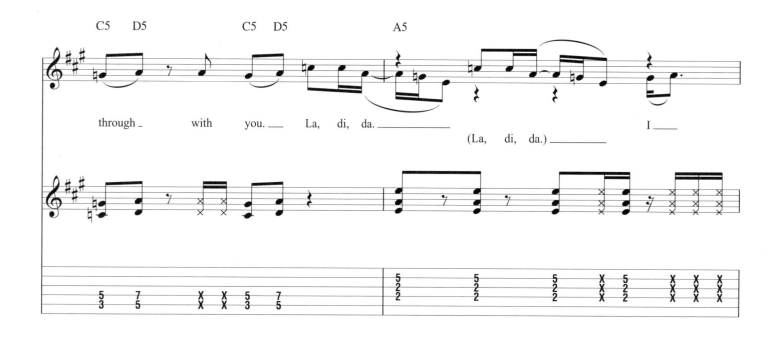

through __ with you. __ La, di, da. _____

(La, di, da.) _____ I ___

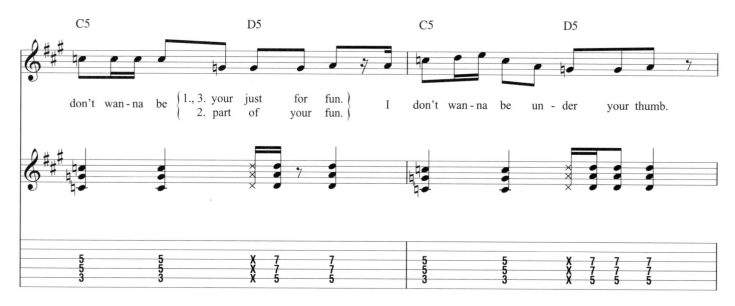

don't wan - na be {1., 3. your just for fun. / 2. part of your fun.} I don't wan - na be un - der your thumb.

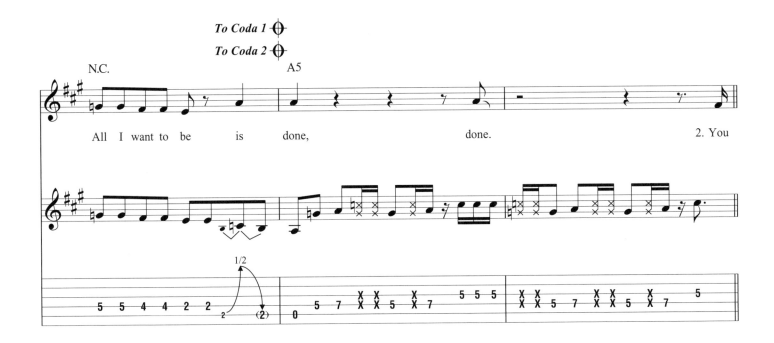

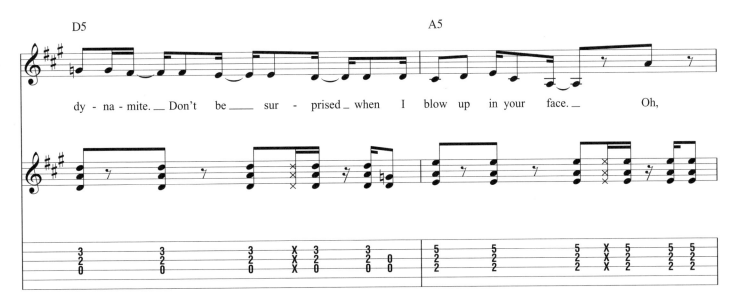

my.   Oh, _____ my. _____   Ha!

w/ slight dist.

$\oplus$ Coda 1

Bridge

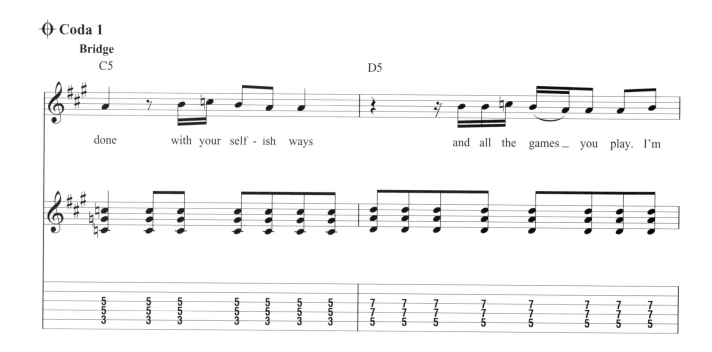

done   with your self - ish ways   and all the games_ you play. I'm

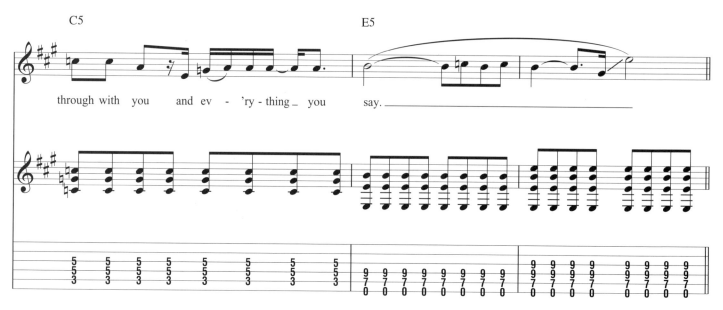

through with you   and ev - 'ry-thing_ you   say. _____

Fiddle Solo

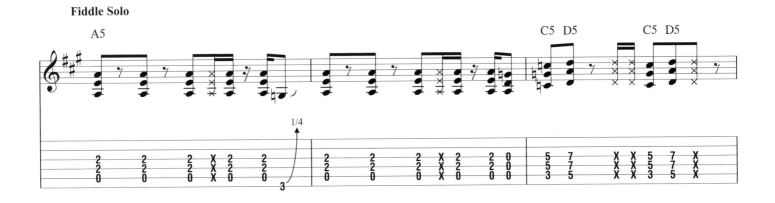

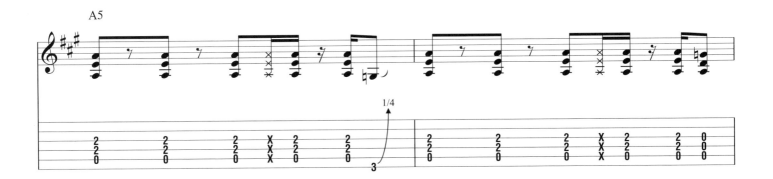

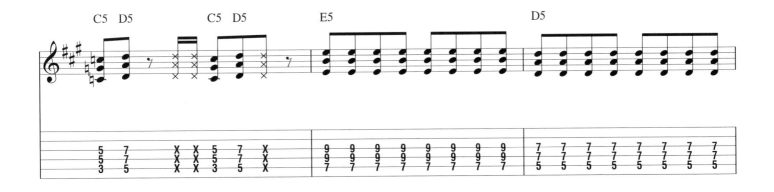

Ma - ma told me that I ____ should play nice. She did - n't know you when she gave _ me that ad - vice.

Coda 2

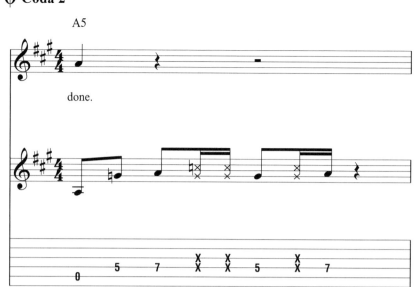

A5

done.

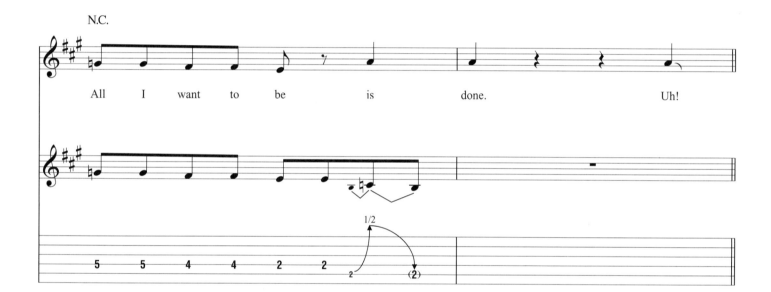

N.C.

All I want to be is done. Uh!

1/2

Outro

A5

Hey, — hey, hey,

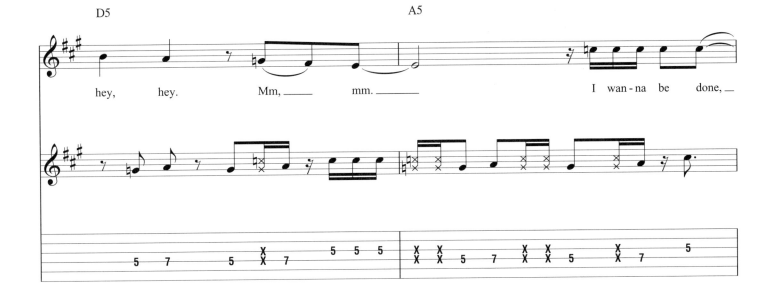

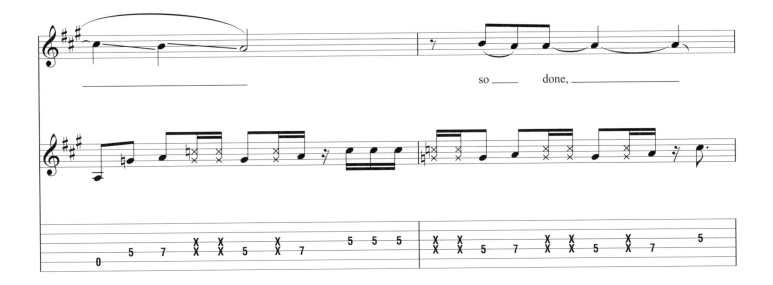

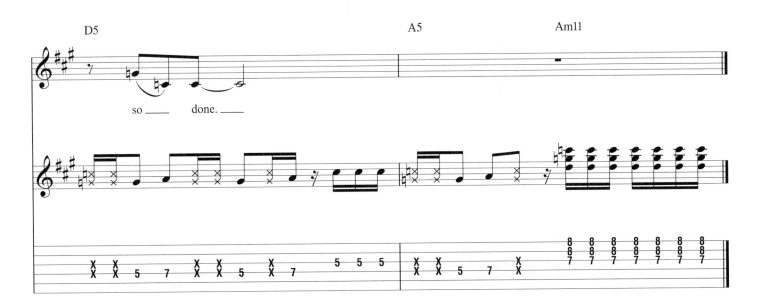

Die a Happy Man

Words and Music by Thomas Rhett, Joe Spargur and Sean Douglas

Intro
Moderately slow ♩ = 83

*Slap muted strings w/ picking hand, throughout.

1. Ba - by,

last night
2. *See additional lyrics*

was hands _____ down, ___ one of the

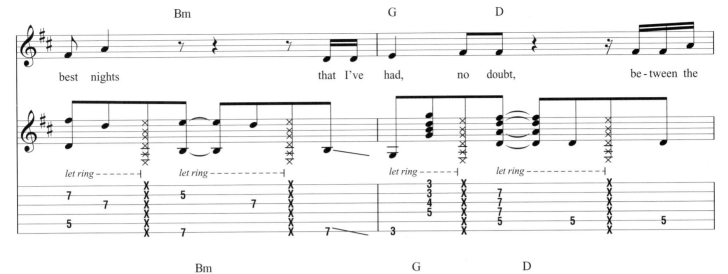

best nights   that I've had,   no doubt,   be - tween the

bot - tle of wine _ and the look in your eyes and the Mar - vin _ Gaye. _   Then we

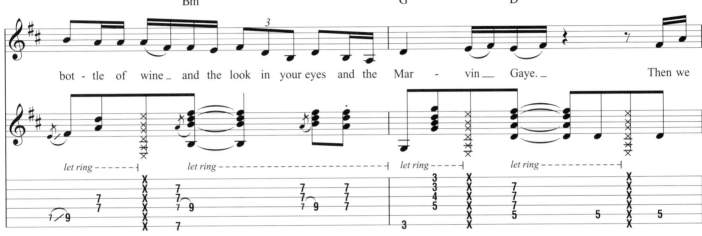

danced in the dark _ un - der Sep - tem - ber stars in the pour - in' rain. _   And I

Pre-Chorus

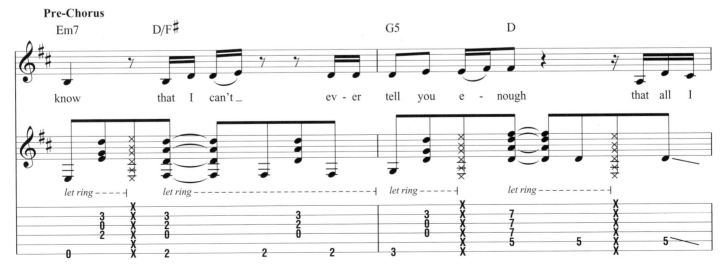

know   that I can't _   ev - er tell you e - nough   that all I

need   in this life ___   is your cra - zy love. ___   If I

let ring   *let ring*

Chorus

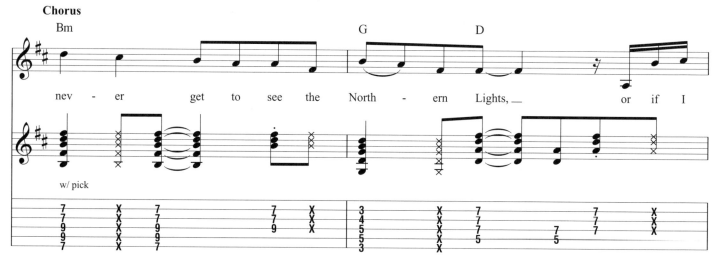

nev - er   get   to   see   the   North - ern   Lights, ___   or if I

w/ pick

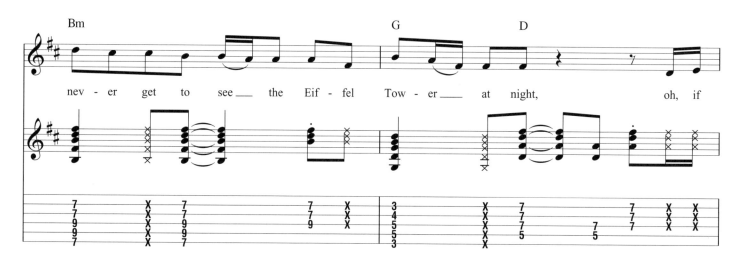

nev - er get to see ___ the Eif - fel Tow - er ___ at night,   oh, if

all   I   got   is   your   hand   in   my   hand,   ba - by,

let ring

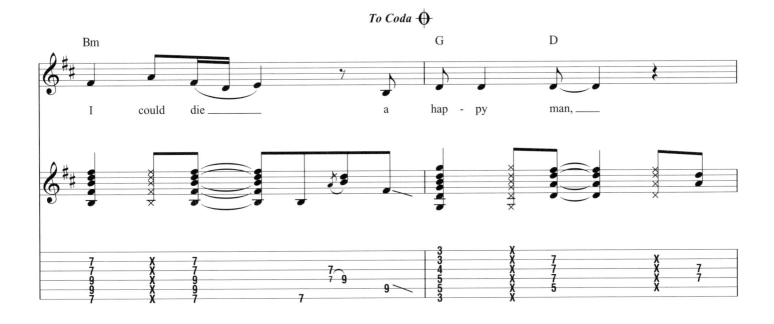

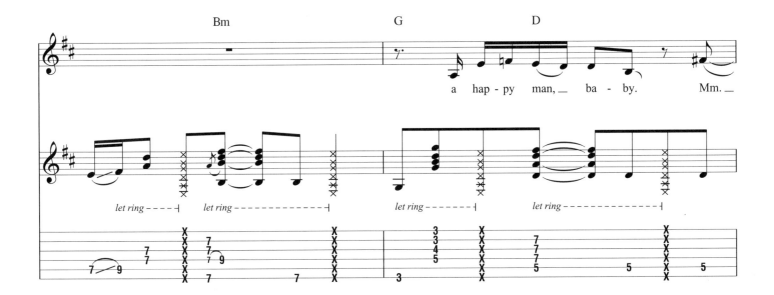

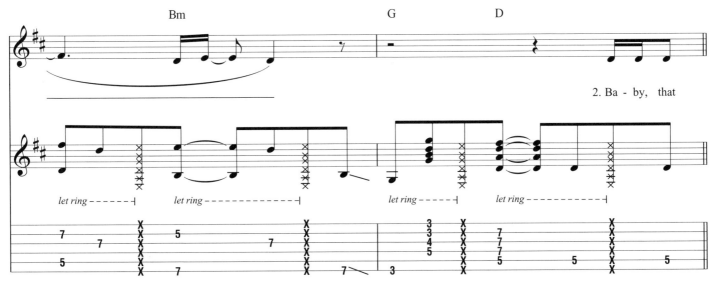

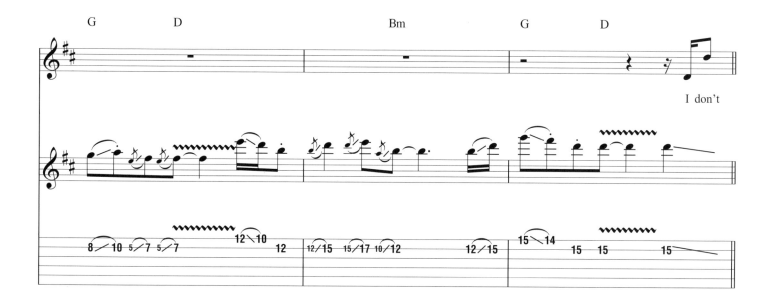

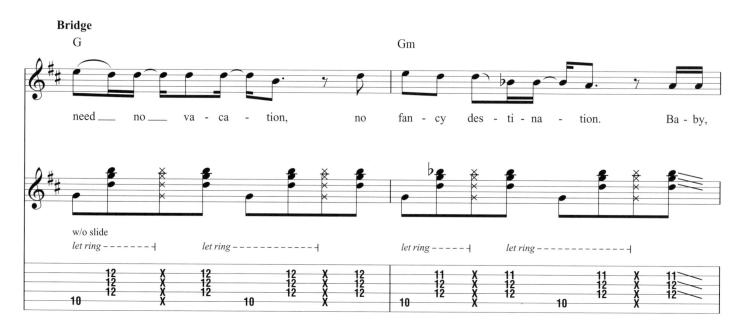

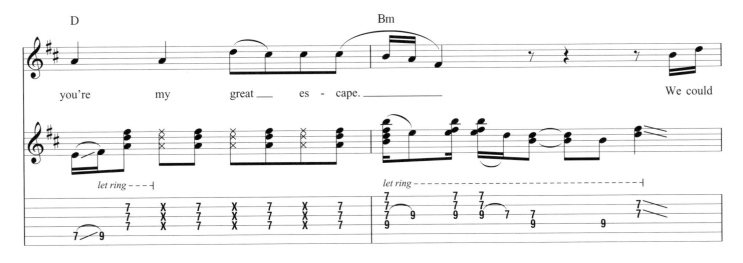

you're my great es - cape. We could

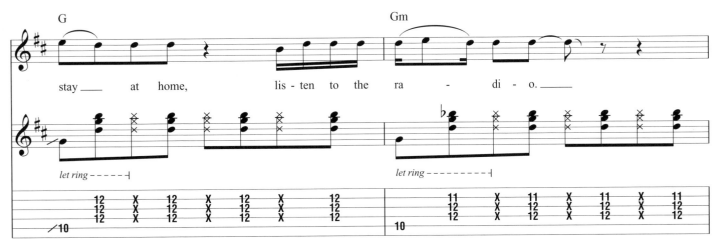

stay at home, lis - ten to the ra - di - o.

dance a - round the fire - place. Oh, if I

Outro-Chorus

nev - er get to build my man - sion in Geor - gia or drive a

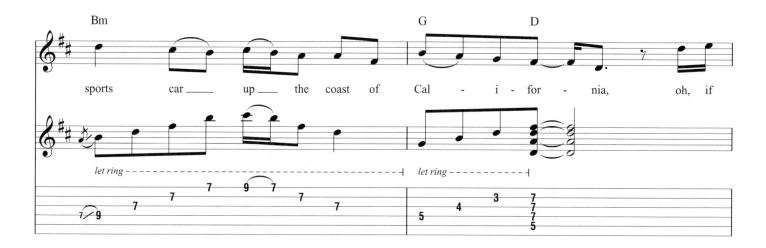

sports car ___ up ___ the coast of Cal - i - for - nia, oh, if

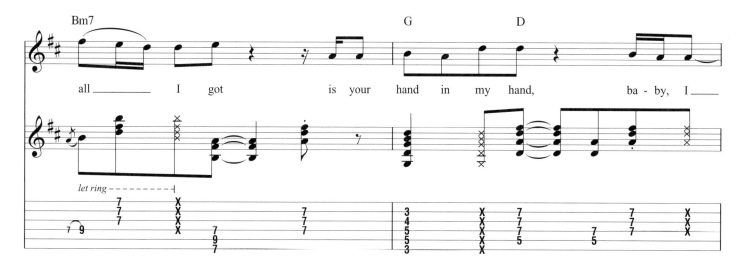

all ___ I got is your hand in my hand, ba - by, I ___

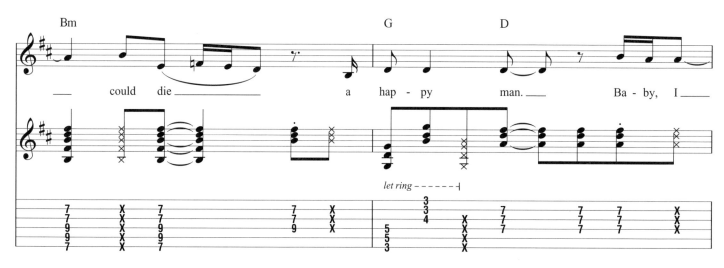

___ could die ___ a hap - py man. ___ Ba - by, I ___

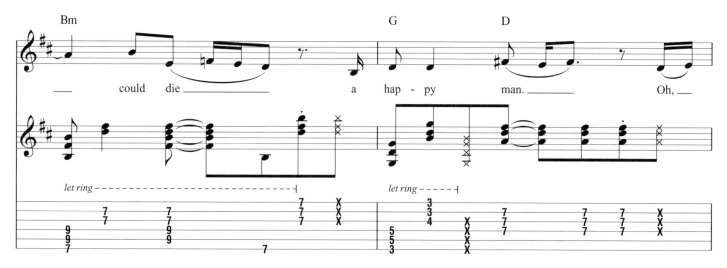

___ could die ___ a hap - py man. ___ Oh, ___

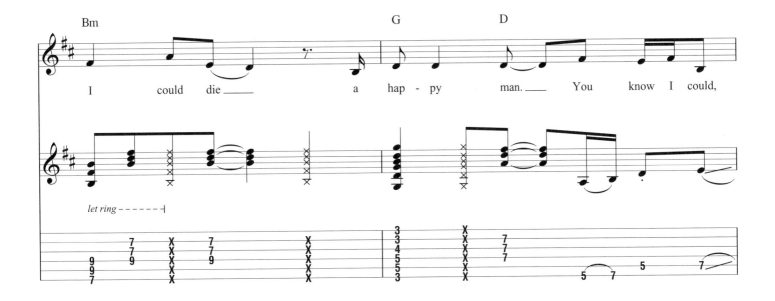

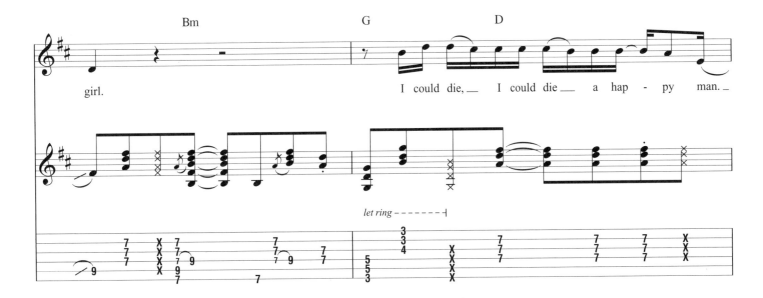

Additional Lyrics

2. Baby, that red dress brings me to my knees.
   Oh, but that black dress makes it hard to breathe.
   You're a saint, you're a goddess. The cutest, the hottest masterpiece.
   It's too good to be true. Nothin' better than you in my wildest dreams.

Drink in My Hand

Words and Music by Eric Church, Michael Heeney and Luke Laird

Capo III

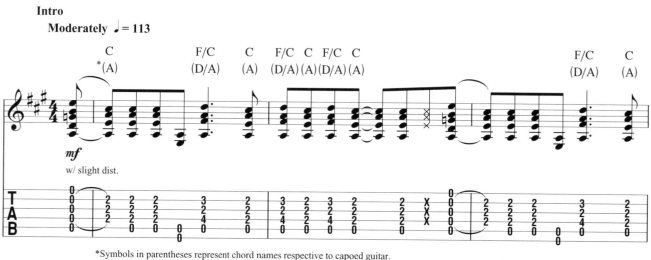

*Symbols in parentheses represent chord names respective to capoed guitar.
Symbols above reflect actual sounding chords. Capoed fret is "0" in tab.

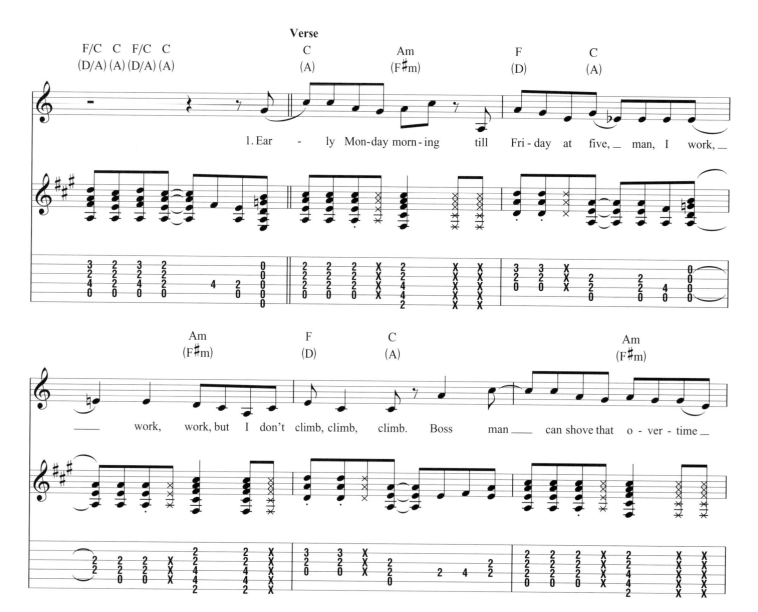

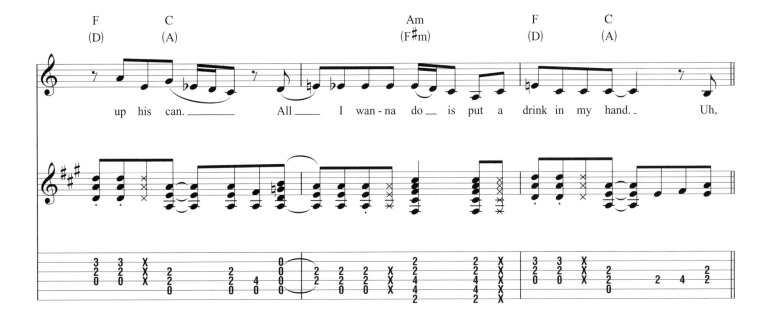

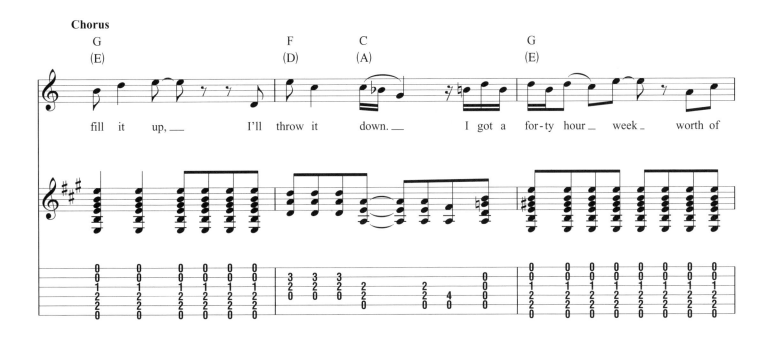

Chorus

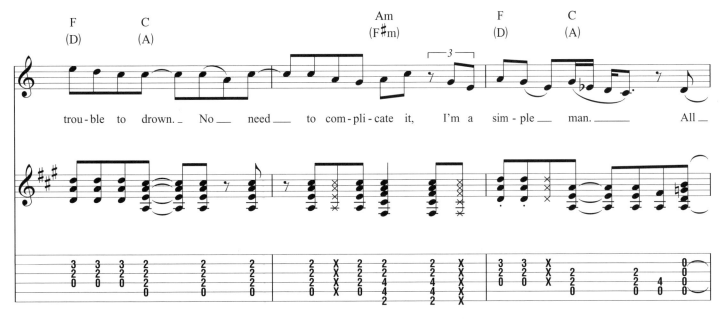

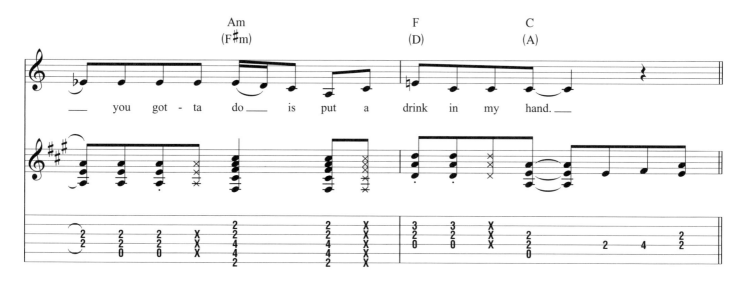

you got-ta do is put a drink in my hand.

Interlude

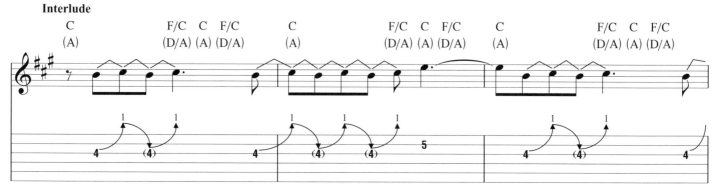

Verse

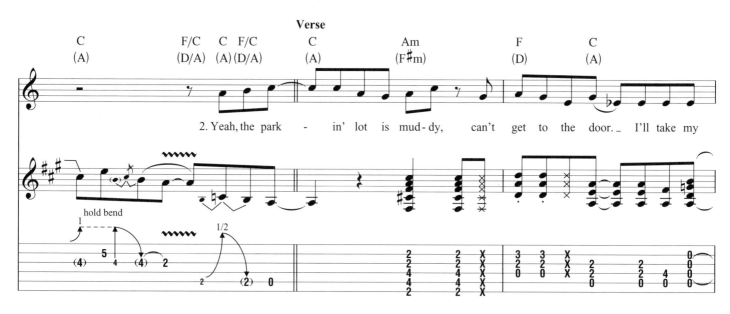

2. Yeah, the park-in' lot is mud-dy, can't get to the door. I'll take my

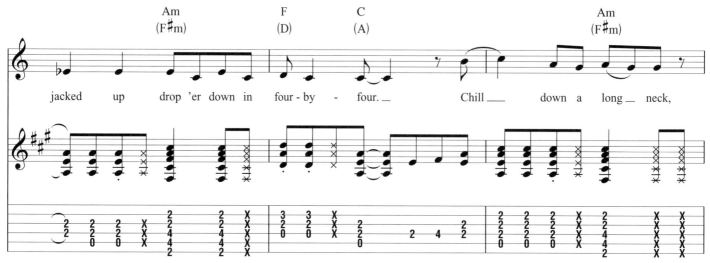

jacked up drop 'er down in four-by-four. Chill down a long neck,

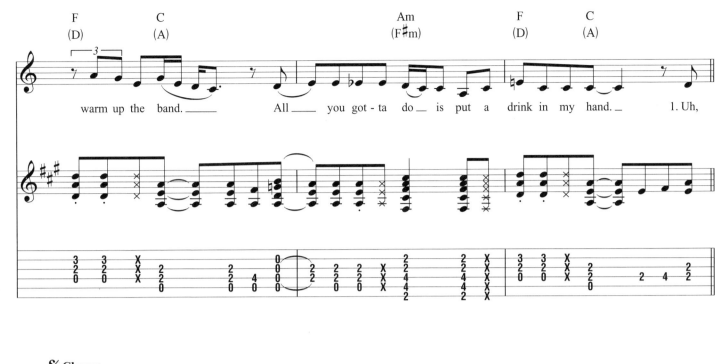

warm up the band. ___ All ___ you got-ta do ___ is put a drink in my hand. ___ 1. Uh,

𝄉 **Chorus**

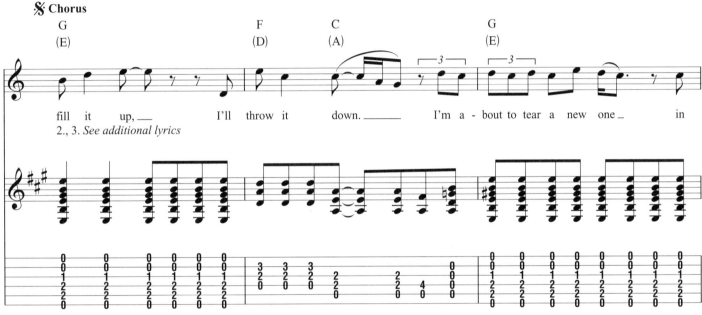

fill it up, ___ I'll throw it down. ___ I'm a-bout to tear a new one ___ in
2., 3. *See additional lyrics*

To Coda 1 ⊕
To Coda 2 ⊕

this old ___ town. ___ Five, _ four, three, two, _ one. _ I'm a rock-et ___ man. ___ All ___

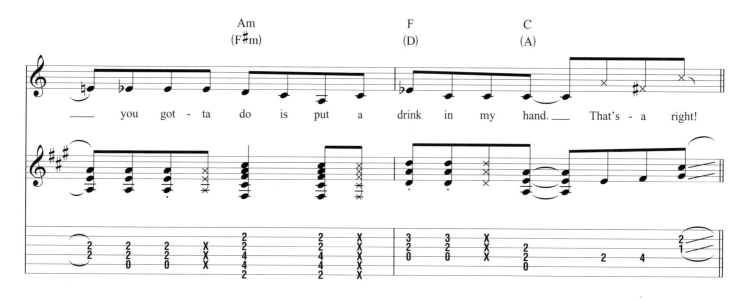

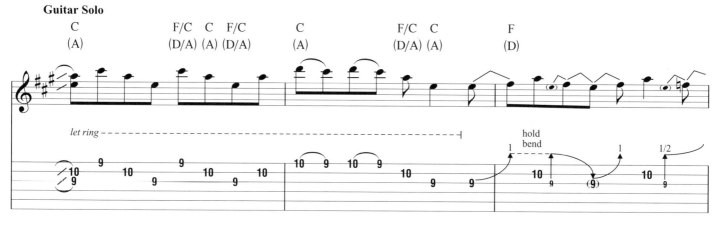

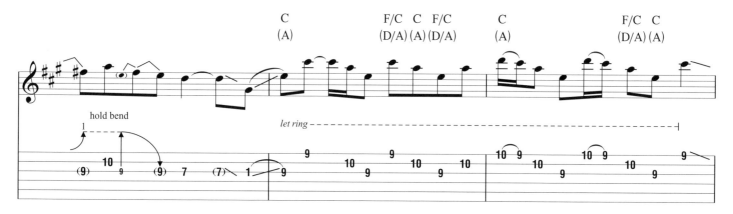

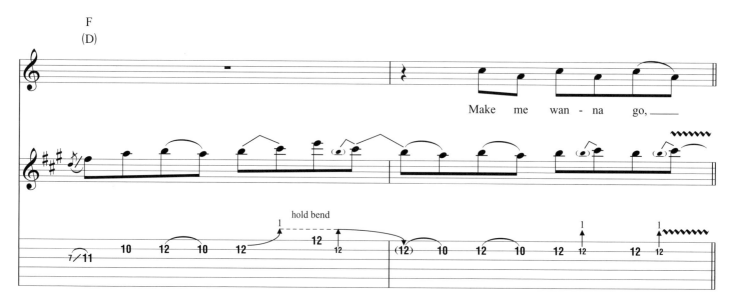

Bridge

"Ooh, _ ooh, _ ooh," _____ when you dance like _ that. _ You got that lit - tle tat - too play-in' _ peek - a -

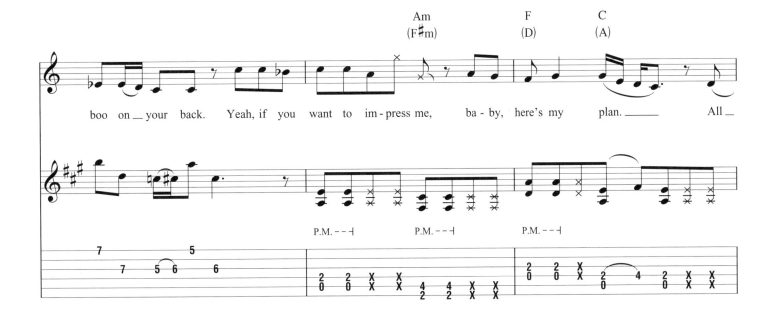

boo on _ your back. Yeah, if you want to im - press me, ba - by, here's my plan. _____ All _

D.S. al Coda 1

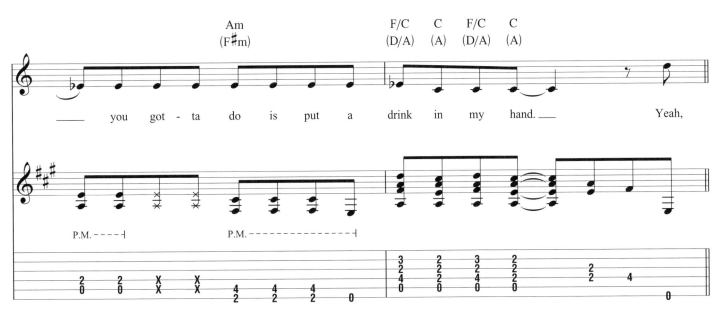

_____ you got - ta do is put a drink in my hand. _____ Yeah,

✢ Coda 1

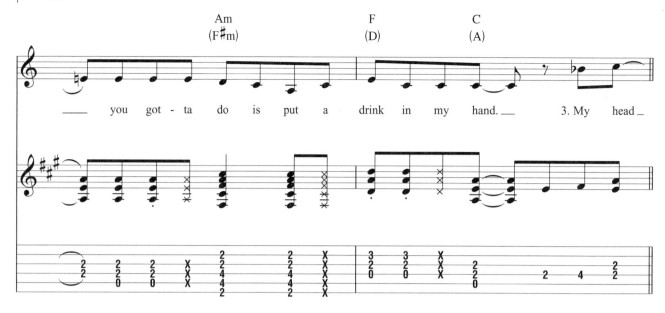

you got-ta do is put a drink in my hand. ___ 3. My head ___

Verse

Mon-day morn-in' that a-larm clock sings, ___ it goes bang, bang, bang ___ while it

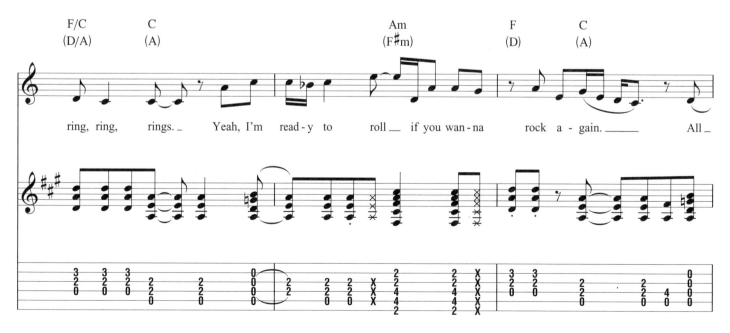

ring, ring, rings. ___ Yeah, I'm read-y to roll ___ if you wan-na rock a-gain. _____ All ___

58

N.C.   F/C   C
(D/A)   (A)

___ you got - ta do is put a drink in my hand. ___ Yeah,

$\oplus$ Coda 2

Am   F   C
(F#m)   (D)   (A)

___ you got - ta do ___ is put a drink in my hand. ___ That

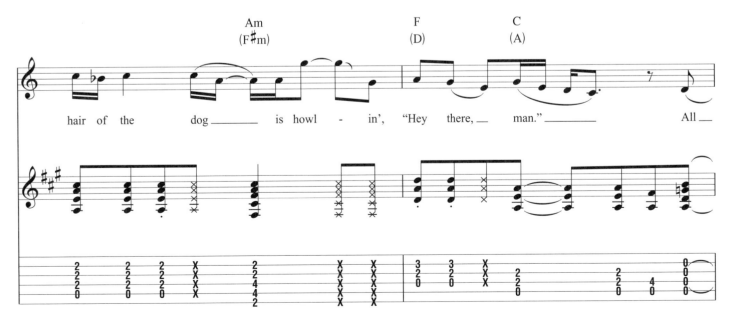

Am   F   C
(F#m)   (D)   (A)

hair of the dog ___ is howl - in', "Hey there, ___ man." _____ All ___

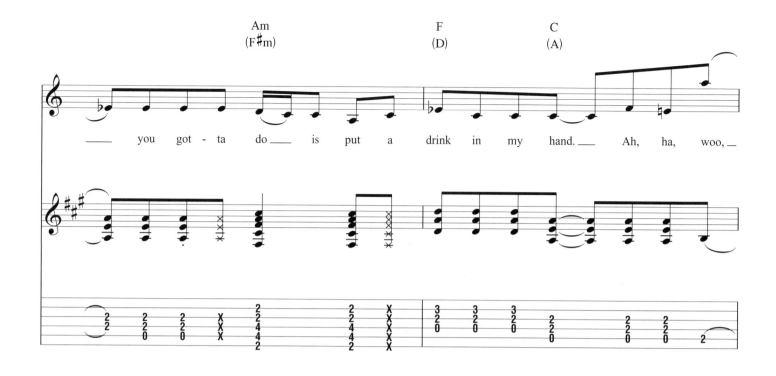

you got - ta do — is put a drink in my hand. — Ah, ha, woo, —

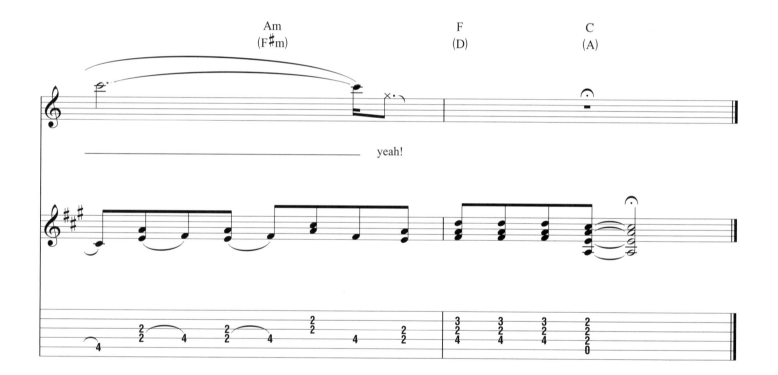

yeah!

Additional Lyrics

Chorus 2. Yeah, fill it up, I'll throw it down.
When you drive me home, take the long way around.
You'll be my Lois Lane, I'll be your Superman.
All you gotta do is put a drink in my hand. That's-a right!

Chorus 3. Yeah, fill it up, I'll throw it down.
I got a little hung over, still hangin' around.
Yeah, that hair of the dog is howlin', "Hey there, man."
All you gotta do is put a drink in my hand.

Wagon Wheel

Words and Music by Bob Dylan and Ketch Secor

Intro
Moderately fast ♩ = 148

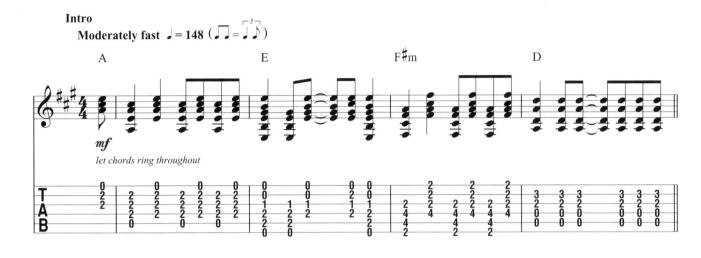

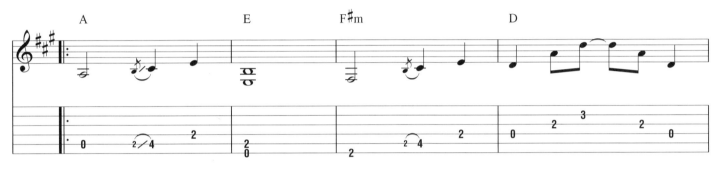

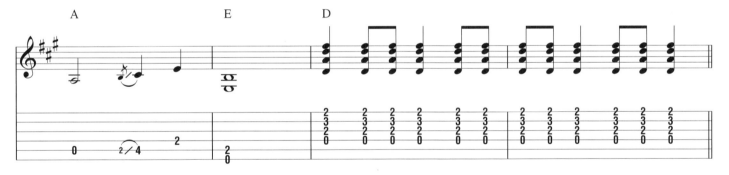

Verse

1. Head-in' down _ south _ to the land _ of the pines, _ I'm thumb-in' my _ way _ in - to North _
2. *See additional lyrics*

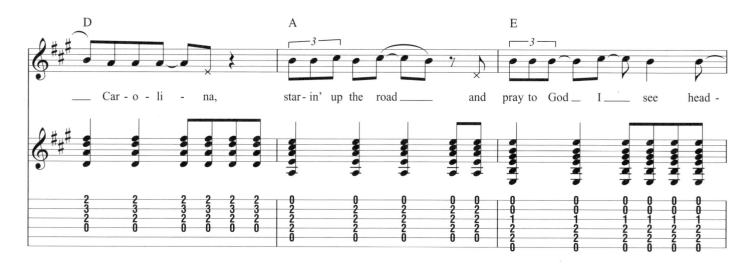

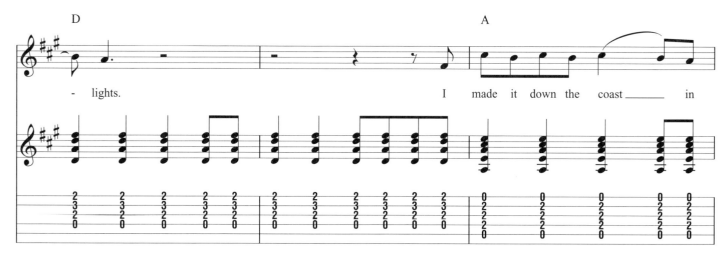

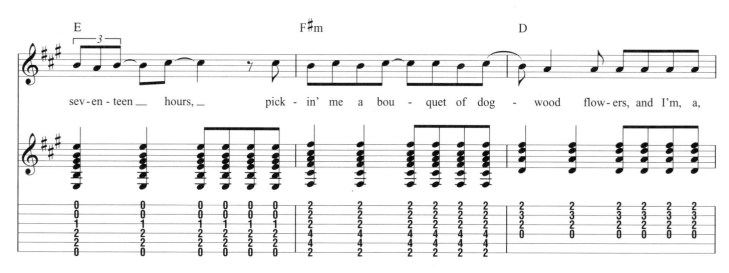

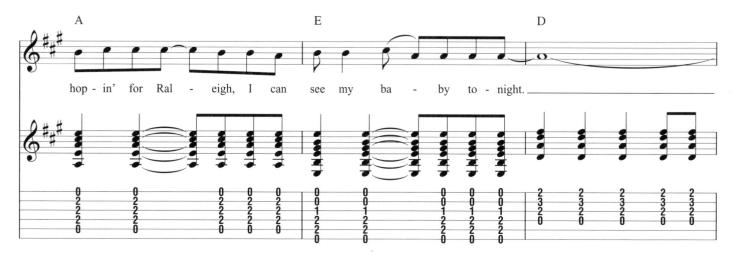

Chorus

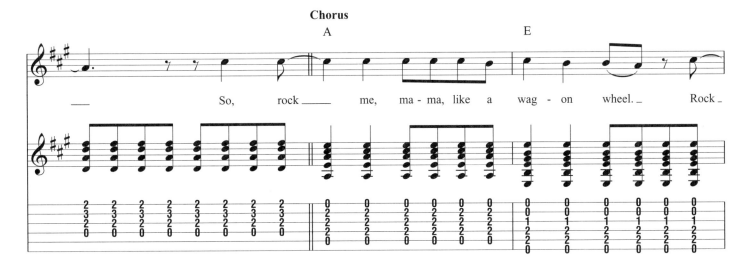

So, rock ___ me, ma - ma, like a wag - on wheel. ___ Rock ___

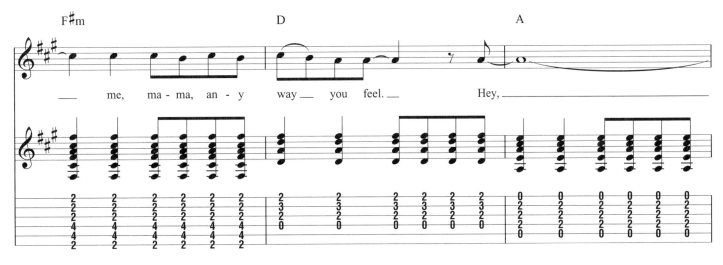

___ me, ma - ma, an - y way ___ you feel. ___ Hey, ___

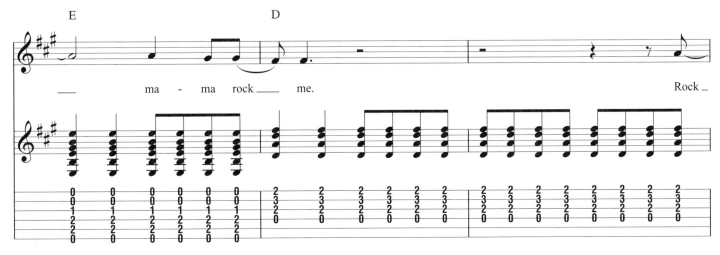

___ ma - ma rock ___ me. Rock ___

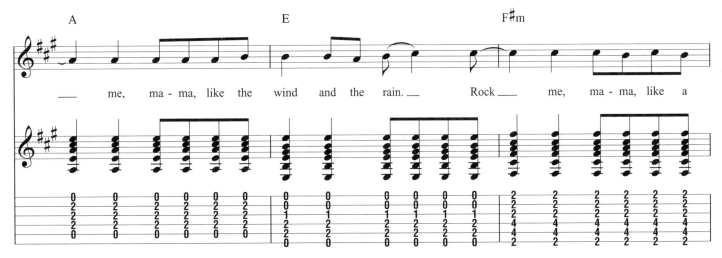

___ me, ma - ma, like the wind and the rain. ___ Rock ___ me, ma - ma, like a

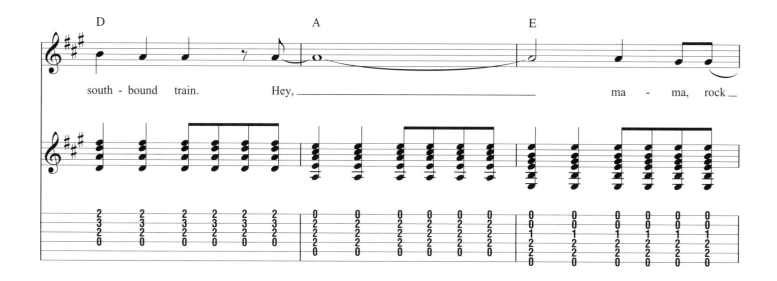

south - bound train. Hey, _____ ma - ma, rock _

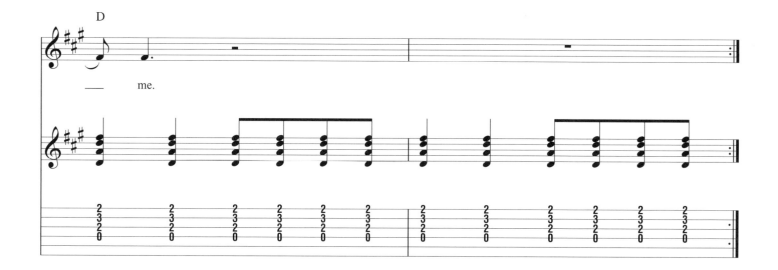

_ me.

Fiddle Solo

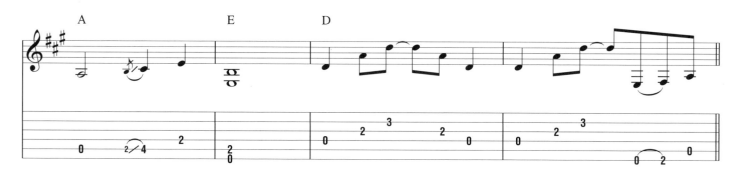

Guitar Solo

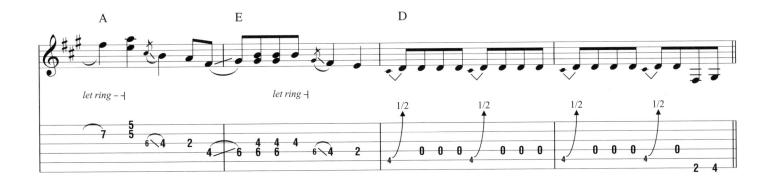

Verse

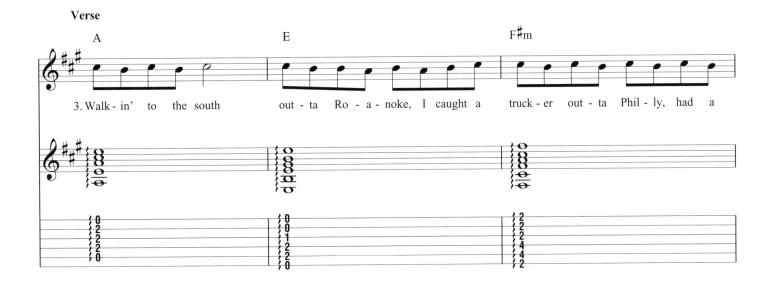

3. Walk-in' to the south out-ta Ro-a-noke, I caught a truck-er out-ta Phil-ly, had a

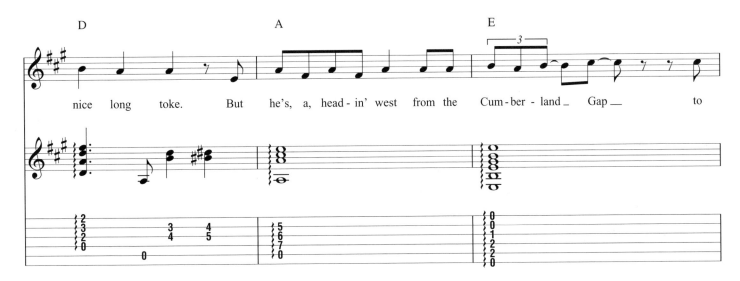

nice long toke. But he's, a, head-in' west from the Cum-ber-land __ Gap __ to

End half-time feel

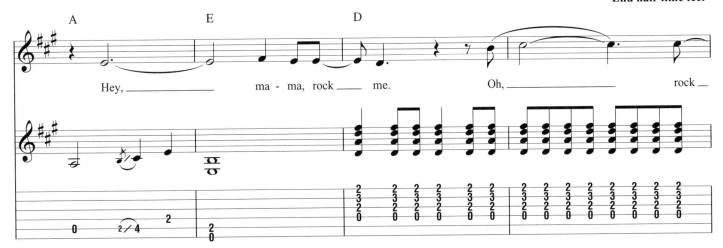

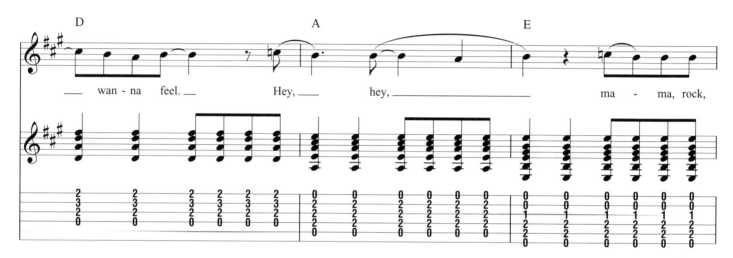

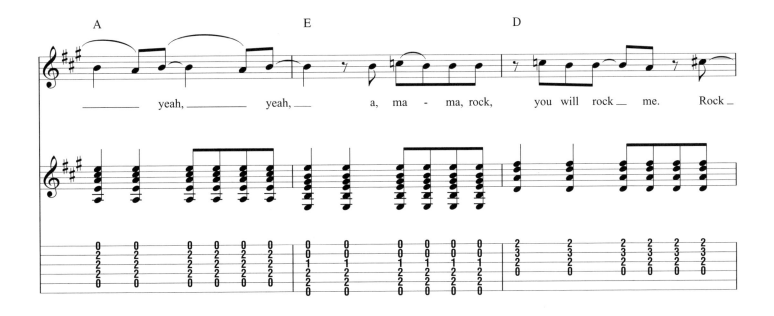

yeah, ____ yeah, ____ a, ma - ma, rock, you will rock __ me. Rock __

Outro

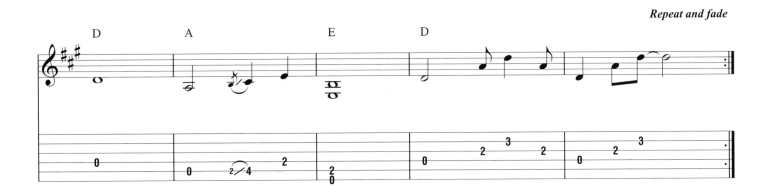

me. _____

*Sung 1st time only.

Repeat and fade

Additional Lyrics

2. I'm runnin' from the cold up in New England,
I was born to be a fiddler in an old-time string band.
My baby plays the guitar; I pick a banjo now.
Oh, north country winters keep, a, gettin' me down.
Lost my money playin' poker so I had to leave town.
But I ain't, a, turnin' back to livin' that old life no more.

Tennessee Whiskey

Words and Music by Dean Dillon and Linda Hargrove

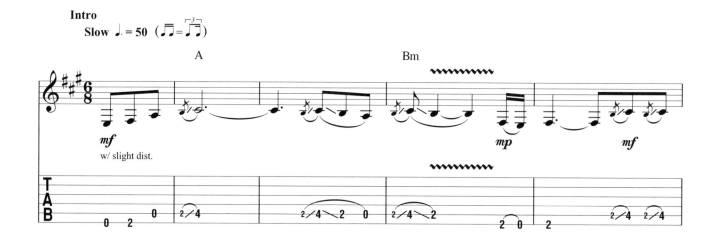

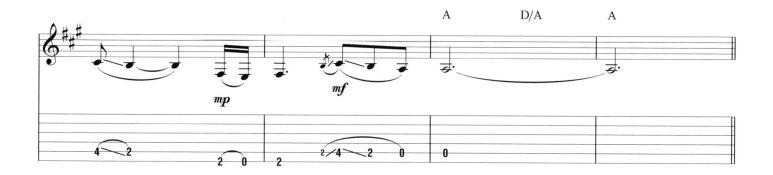

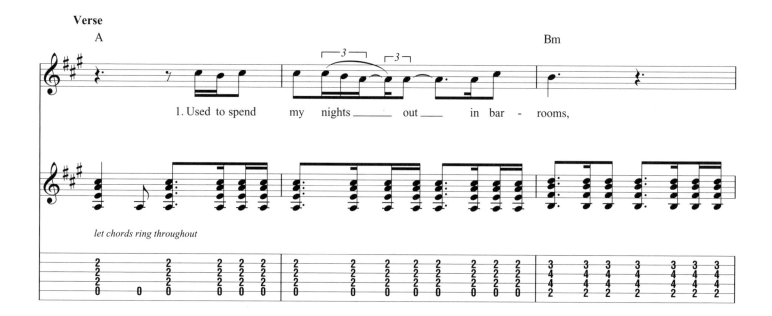

liq - uor was   the on - ly love _____ I'd   known. _____

*Sung as even sixteenth notes.

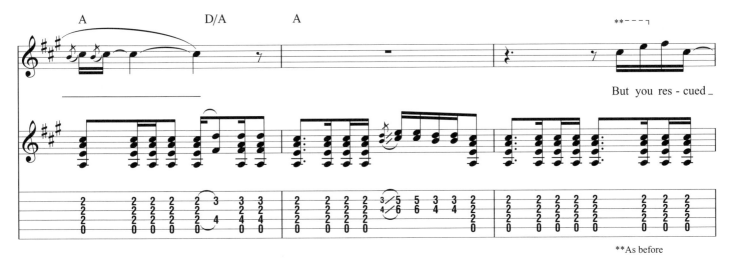

A   D/A   A

But you res - cued _

**As before

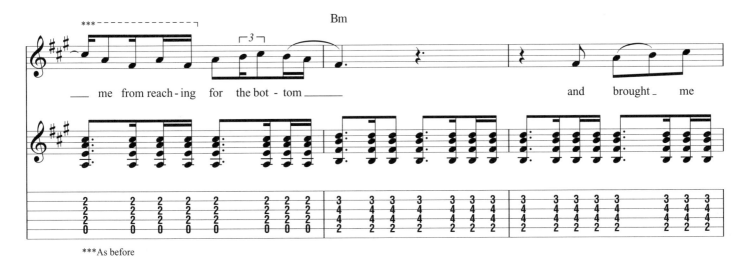

Bm

_____ me from reach - ing for the bot - tom _____   and   brought _ me

***As before

A   D/A

back   from be - ing too far gone. _____

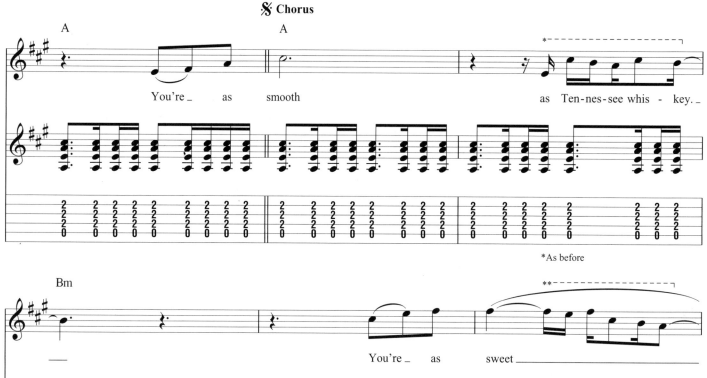

*As before

**As before

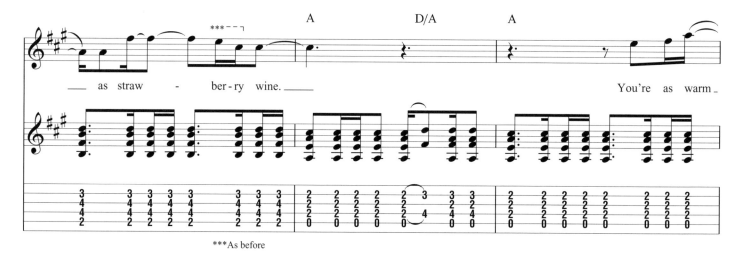

***As before

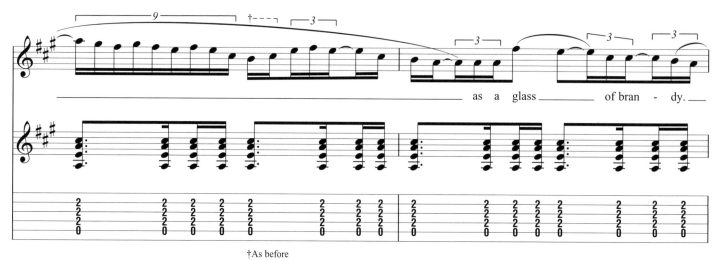

†As before

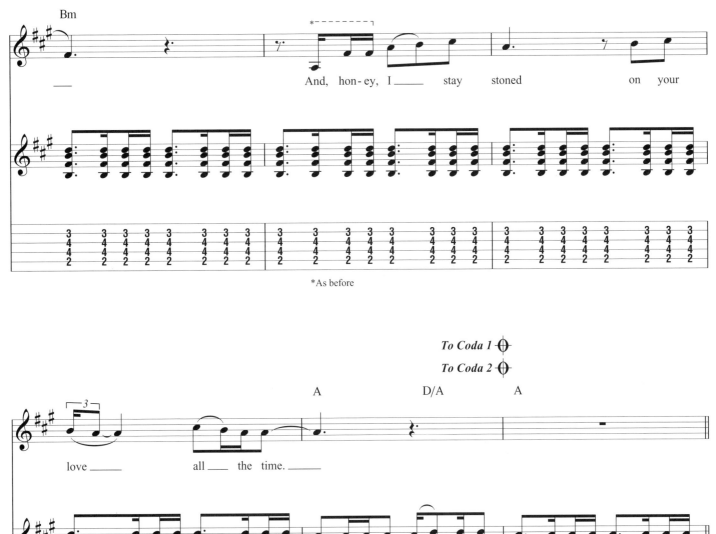

*As before

To Coda 1 ⊕
To Coda 2 ⊕

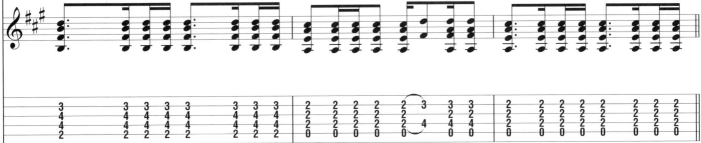

**As before

found the bot - tom

*As before

A   D/A   A

of the bot-tle's al - ways dry.

**But when you poured out your heart I did-n't waste

**As before

Bm

it   'cause there's noth - ing   like your

***As before

74

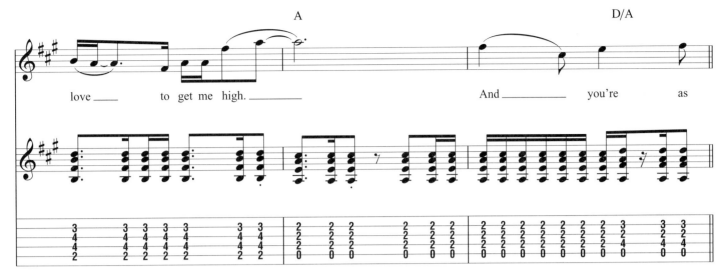

love _____ to get me high. _____ And _____ you're as

⊕ Coda 1

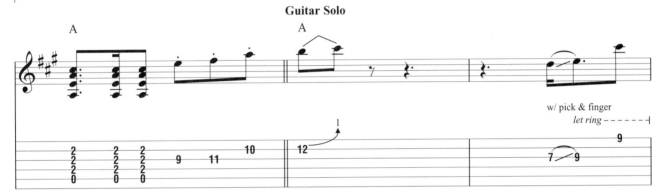

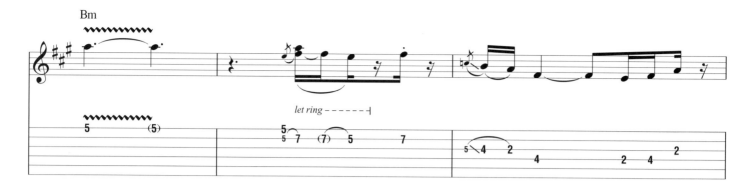

D.S. al Coda 2

You're ___ as

You're ___ as smooth ___

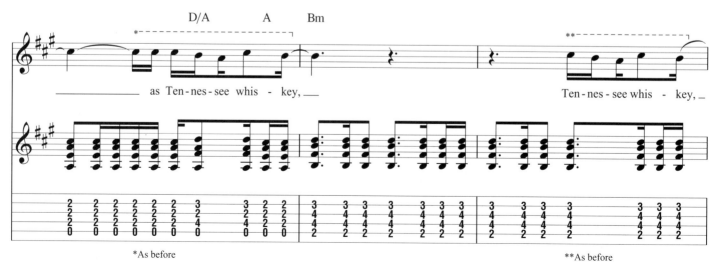

___ as Ten-nes-see whis - key, ___

Ten-nes-see whis - key, ___

*As before

**As before

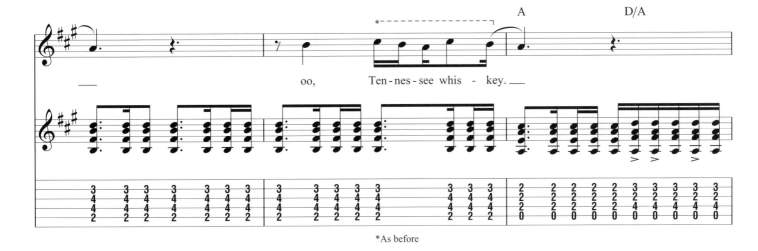

oo, Ten - nes - see whis - key. ___

*As before

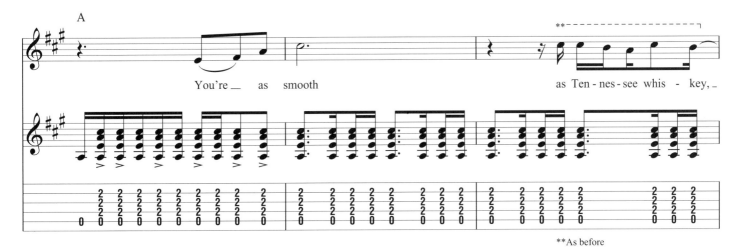

You're ___ as smooth   as Ten - nes - see whis - key, ___

**As before

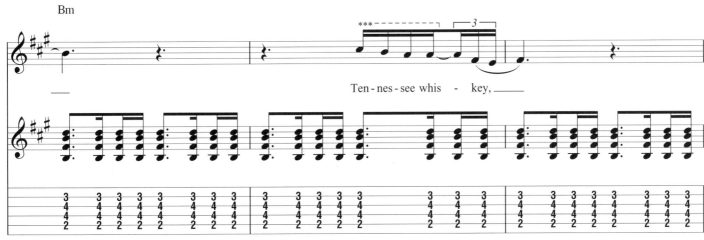

Ten - nes - see whis - key, ___

***As before

Free time

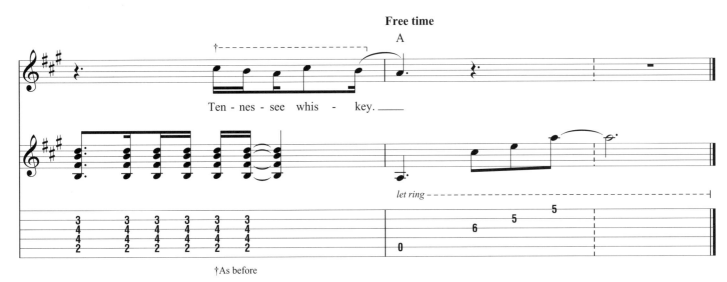

Ten - nes - see whis - key. ___

let ring -

†As before

Hal•Leonard® GUITAR PLAY-ALONG

AUDIO ACCESS INCLUDED

INCLUDES TAB

This series will help you play your favorite songs quickly and easily. Just follow the tab and listen to the CD or online audio to hear how the guitar should sound, and then play along using the separate backing tracks. Playback tools are provided for slowing down the tempo without changing pitch and looping challenging parts. The melody and lyrics are included in the book so that you can sing or simply follow along.

85. THE POLICE
00700269....................$16.99

86. BOSTON
00700465....................$16.99

87. ACOUSTIC WOMEN
00700763....................$14.99

88. GRUNGE
00700467....................$16.99

89. REGGAE
00700468....................$15.99

90. CLASSICAL POP
00700469....................$14.99

91. BLUES INSTRUMENTALS
00700505....................$15.99

92. EARLY ROCK INSTRUMENTALS
00700506....................$15.99

93. ROCK INSTRUMENTALS
00700507....................$16.99

94. SLOW BLUES
00700508....................$16.99

95. BLUES CLASSICS
00700509....................$14.99

97. CHRISTMAS CLASSICS
00236542....................$14.99

98. ROCK BAND
00700704....................$14.95

99. ZZ TOP
00700762....................$16.99

100. B.B. KING
00700466....................$16.99

101. SONGS FOR BEGINNERS
00701917....................$14.99

102. CLASSIC PUNK
00700769....................$14.99

103. SWITCHFOOT
00700773....................$16.99

104. DUANE ALLMAN
00700846....................$16.99

105. LATIN
00700939....................$16.99

106. WEEZER
00700958....................$14.99

107. CREAM
00701069....................$16.99

108. THE WHO
00701053....................$16.99

109. STEVE MILLER
00701054....................$16.99

110. SLIDE GUITAR HITS
00701055....................$16.99

111. JOHN MELLENCAMP
00701056....................$14.99

112. QUEEN
00701052....................$16.99

113. JIM CROCE
00701058....................$16.99

114. BON JOVI
00701060....................$16.99

115. JOHNNY CASH
00701070....................$16.99

116. THE VENTURES
00701124....................$16.99

117. BRAD PAISLEY
00701224....................$16.99

118. ERIC JOHNSON
00701353....................$16.99

119. AC/DC CLASSICS
00701356....................$17.99

120. PROGRESSIVE ROCK
00701457....................$14.99

121. U2
00701508....................$16.99

122. CROSBY, STILLS & NASH
00701610....................$16.99

123. LENNON & McCARTNEY ACOUSTIC
00701614....................$16.99

125. JEFF BECK
00701687....................$16.99

126. BOB MARLEY
00701701....................$16.99

127. 1970S ROCK
00701739....................$16.99

128. 1960S ROCK
00701740....................$14.99

129. MEGADETH
00701741....................$16.99

130. IRON MAIDEN
00701742....................$17.99

131. 1990S ROCK
00701743....................$14.99

132. COUNTRY ROCK
00701757....................$15.99

133. TAYLOR SWIFT
00701894....................$16.99

134. AVENGED SEVENFOLD
00701906....................$16.99

135. MINOR BLUES
00151350....................$17.99

136. GUITAR THEMES
00701922....................$14.99

137. IRISH TUNES
00701966....................$15.99

138. BLUEGRASS CLASSICS
00701967....................$14.99

139. GARY MOORE
00702370....................$16.99

140. MORE STEVIE RAY VAUGHAN
00702396....................$17.99

141. ACOUSTIC HITS
00702401....................$16.99

143. SLASH
00702425....................$19.99

144. DJANGO REINHARDT
00702531....................$16.99

145. DEF LEPPARD
00702532....................$17.99

146. ROBERT JOHNSON
00702533....................$16.99

147. SIMON & GARFUNKEL
14041591....................$16.99

148. BOB DYLAN
14041592....................$16.99

149. AC/DC HITS
14041593....................$17.99

150. ZAKK WYLDE
02501717....................$16.99

151. J.S. BACH
02501730....................$16.99

152. JOE BONAMASSA
02501751....................$19.99

153. RED HOT CHILI PEPPERS
00702990....................$19.99

155. ERIC CLAPTON – FROM THE ALBUM UNPLUGGED
00703085....................$16.99

156. SLAYER
00703770....................$17.99

157. FLEETWOOD MAC
00101382....................$16.99

158. ULTIMATE CHRISTMAS
00101889....................$14.99

159. WES MONTGOMERY
00102593....................$19.99

160. T-BONE WALKER
00102641....................$16.99

161. THE EAGLES – ACOUSTIC
00102659....................$17.99

162. THE EAGLES HITS
00102667....................$17.99

163. PANTERA
00103036....................$17.99

164. VAN HALEN 1986-1995
00110270....................$17.99

165. GREEN DAY
00210343....................$17.99

166. MODERN BLUES
00700764....................$16.99

167. DREAM THEATER
00111938....................$24.99

168. KISS
00113421....................$16.99

169. TAYLOR SWIFT
00115982....................$16.99

170. THREE DAYS GRACE
00117337....................$16.99

171. JAMES BROWN
00117420....................$16.99

173. TRANS-SIBERIAN ORCHESTRA
00119907....................$19.99

174. SCORPIONS
00122119....................$16.99

175. MICHAEL SCHENKER
00122127....................$16.99

176. BLUES BREAKERS WITH JOHN MAYALL & ERIC CLAPTON
00122132....................$19.99

177. ALBERT KING
00123271....................$16.99

178. JASON MRAZ
00124165....................$17.99

179. RAMONES
00127073....................$16.99

180. BRUNO MARS
00129706....................$16.99

181. JACK JOHNSON
00129854....................$16.99

182. SOUNDGARDEN
00138161....................$17.99

183. BUDDY GUY
00138240....................$17.99

184. KENNY WAYNE SHEPHERD
00138258....................$17.99

185. JOE SATRIANI
00139457....................$17.99

186. GRATEFUL DEAD
00139459....................$17.99

187. JOHN DENVER
00140839....................$17.99

188. MÖTLEY CRUE
00141145....................$17.99

189. JOHN MAYER
00144350....................$17.99

191. PINK FLOYD CLASSICS
00146164....................$17.99

192. JUDAS PRIEST
00151352....................$17.99

For complete songlists, visit Hal Leonard online at
www.halleonard.com

Prices, contents, and availability subject to change without notice.

DELUXE GUITAR PLAY-ALONG

AUDIO ACCESS INCLUDED 🔊

The Deluxe Guitar Play-Along series will help you play songs faster than ever before! Accurate, easy-to-read guitar tab and professional, customizable audio for 15 songs. The interactive, online audio interface includes tempo/pitch control, looping, buttons to turn instruments on or off, and guitar tab with follow-along marker. The price of each book includes access to audio tracks online using the unique code inside. The tracks can also be downloaded and played offline. Now including PLAYBACK+, a multi-functional audio player that allows you to slow down audio, change pitch, set loop points, and pan left or right – available exclusively from Hal Leonard.

1. TOP ROCK HITS
Basket Case • Black Hole Sun • Come As You Are • Do I Wanna Know? • Gold on the Ceiling • Heaven • How You Remind Me • Kryptonite • No One Knows • Plush • The Pretender • Seven Nation Army • Smooth • Under the Bridge • Yellow Ledbetter.

00244758 Book/Online Audio $19.99

2. REALLY EASY SONGS
All the Small Things • Brain Stew • Californication • Free Fallin' • Helter Skelter • Hey Joe • Highway to Hell • Hurt (Quiet) • I Love Rock 'N Roll • Island in the Sun • Knockin' on Heaven's Door • La Bamba • Oh, Pretty Woman • Should I Stay or Should I Go • Smells Like Teen Spirit.

00244877 Book/Online Audio $19.99

3. ACOUSTIC SONGS
All Apologies • Banana Pancakes • Crash Into Me • Good Riddance (Time of Your Life) • Hallelujah • Hey There Delilah • Ho Hey • I Will Wait • I'm Yours • Iris • More Than Words • No Such Thing • Photograph • What I Got • Wonderwall.

00244709 Book/Online Audio $19.99

4. THE BEATLES
All My Loving • And I Love Her • Back in the U.S.S.R. • Don't Let Me Down • Get Back • A Hard Day's Night • Here Comes the Sun • I Will • In My Life • Let It Be • Michelle • Paperback Writer • Revolution • While My Guitar Gently Weeps • Yesterday.

00244968 Book/Online Audio $19.99

5. BLUES STANDARDS
Baby, What You Want Me to Do • Crosscut Saw • Double Trouble • Every Day I Have the Blues • Going Down • I'm Tore Down • I'm Your Hoochie Coochie Man • If You Love Me Like You Say • Just Your Fool • Killing Floor • Let Me Love You Baby • Messin' with the Kid • Pride and Joy • (They Call It) Stormy Monday (Stormy Monday Blues) • Sweet Home Chicago.

00245090 Book/Online Audio $19.99

6. RED HOT CHILI PEPPERS
The Adventures of Rain Dance Maggie • Breaking the Girl • Can't Stop • Dani California • Dark Necessities • Give It Away • My Friends • Otherside • Road Trippin' • Scar Tissue • Snow (Hey Oh) • Suck My Kiss • Tell Me Baby • Under the Bridge • The Zephyr Song.

00245089 Book/Online Audio $19.99

7. CLASSIC ROCK
Baba O'Riley • Born to Be Wild • Comfortably Numb • Dream On • Fortunate Son • Heartbreaker • Hotel California • Jet Airliner • More Than a Feeling • Old Time Rock & Roll • Rhiannon • Runnin' Down a Dream • Start Me Up • Sultans of Swing • Sweet Home Alabama.

00248381 Book/Online Audio $19.99

8. OZZY OSBOURNE
Bark at the Moon • Close My Eyes Forever • Crazy Train • Dreamer • Goodbye to Romance • I Don't Know • I Don't Wanna Stop • Mama, I'm Coming Home • Miracle Man • Mr. Crowley • No More Tears • Over the Mountain • Perry Mason • Rock 'N Roll Rebel • Shot in the Dark.

00248413 Book/Online Audio $19.99

9. ED SHEERAN
The A Team • All of the Stars • Castle on the Hill • Don't • Drunk • Galway Girl • Give Me Love • How Would You Feel (Paean) • I See Fire • Lego House • Make It Rain • Perfect • Photograph • Shape of You • Thinking Out Loud.

00248439 Book/Online Audio $19.99

HAL•LEONARD®
www.halleonard.com